A Life like No Other

BERNICE BONILLA

PAGE PUBLISHING, INC.
Conneaut Lake, PA

First originally published by Page Publishing 2020

ISBN 978-1-64701-559-6 (pbk)
ISBN 978-1-64701-560-2 (digital)

Printed in the United States of America

It's Time to Move On

"Good night. Thank you so much for coming. I'm so happy you were able to come and celebrate this big undertaking with me. I can't believe I'm actually retiring," I repeated over and over to my friends, coworkers and family who came to my retirement party at the Highland Lakes Firehouse. The party was over, and it was time for me to leave.

As I climbed into the car with my husband, Pete, I said, "Well, it's official. Once you have the party, there's no going back." I laughed. I hoped I did the right thing. As we drove away, the questions started playing on in my mind:

Did I jump into this decision too early?
What will I do?
Can we afford it?

As I tried desperately to quiet the mounting questions, I drifted back into my memories.

"Hey, Mom, you should see this lady came to our shorthand class today, and she had this little machine. You type on these little keys, and it comes out on this strip of paper. It was so cool. It's called a stenographic machine. They use it in court to take down everything that is said, I want to go to court reporting school," I said, with an excitement that I hadn't ever felt before. I just knew this was what I wanted to do the rest of my life. After all, the only A I ever got on my report card other than gym was in law, and I knew I would never be able to be a lawyer, so this was the next best thing, right?

"Are you kidding me? You hate school and are barely making it out of high school," she said. "Besides, with seven other mouths to feed, there's no money for you to go to school. You need to get a job right after graduation."

1971

"Guess what, I just read a want ad for a file clerk in Hoboken, Beverly," my friend said as I pondered about my future employment.

"I have already been on twelve job interviews and still have not gotten a job. Who knows, do you think thirteen could be my lucky number? Bernadette got the first job she went for. I thought twins were supposed to be alike," I said. "What a joke."

Putting her arm around my shoulder, Beverly continued, "Well, come on, call for an interview. I'll come with you. I'll be your lucky charm."

"I guess it is true thirteen is my lucky number," I said. "I got the job. Could you believe it! Come on, let's get lunch. I'll pay. You can take me to lunch once you get your first paycheck. Wow, I am going to be paid $85 a week. I'm going to save for a car and buy new clothes, and I will be paying board to my mom. I'm so excited."

"You haven't even started yet, and you are already spending your money." Beverly laughed. "When do you start?"

On September 7, 1971, I was so excited. I was at the job at New Jersey Machine in Hoboken, New Jersey, even before the doors opened. Navy-blue skirt and light-blue blouse I borrowed from my older sister Mary who was five years older and convinced me that it brought out the blue of my eyes. I was not even sure what the duties of a file clerk was going to be, but I did have a little office experience from when I was fifteen, when I worked at Housing Authority, alongside Bernadette; it was a program for low-income families for teenagers to work during summer. I guess they thought it was a good idea to have the twins work together. Not sure I agreed, but she did fix my mistakes a few times without anyone in the office catching on, so I guess I should have been grateful.

Well, now I was on my own, my first "big girl job." Mrs. Virgunas walked me into this large room with about seven girls; there was four Dictaphone typist, an addressograph operator, and a secretary to the president and another secretary to vice president. She explained they were a packaging firm where they made machinery to assist in packaging products for manufacturing companies.

I couldn't wait to get started. It took about an hour between filling out all the paperwork and taking a tour of not only the offices and meeting everyone from the different departments, but she also took me through the factory and showed me some of the machines so I would be able to recognize the names when I would be filing. It was so very interesting. The way I felt about the job and constantly talking about it at home, you would have thought I was the president myself. Time flew as I worked to keep the filing up to date but even more important than the work, I met some of the most wonderful people whom I became friends with. These friends became like family to me and were so essential to my well-being. I learned how to run a switchboard and met people from many different states while they would come in for meetings. Within a year, my relationship with my high school sweetheart became quite serious; as a matter of fact, in late September 1972, I found out I was pregnant.

My situation was not too good at home. I was one of ten children, and my dad had died unexpectedly when Bernadette and I were just ten. There were six children still living at home at that time, and my mom was forced to go to work as a nurse's aide at Christ Hospital. It was there she met other widows who would often stop at the local bar to have a drink or two after their long shifts at the hospital. After a couple of years between the stress of raising us and having four teenagers driving her to wit's end, her drinking got out of hand, and she became an alcoholic.

On the night before Thanksgiving, I was so excited; it was the night I decided on telling my mom she was going to be a grandmother for the tenth time. The excitement was building also because all my nine brothers and sisters and their spouses, as well as all the grandchildren, would be over for dinner for Thanksgiving, giving me the opportunity to make my announcement to everyone at one time.

I was eighteen years old, and I had a full-time job, and my boyfriend, Dave, whom I had been dating since I was a freshman in high school, was also working. I assumed she would be happy for us.

"Hey, Mom," I began, "guess what, Dave and I want to get married."

Her response was everything I thought it would not be: "You're too young. You haven't even lived yet. You never even had another boyfriend or experienced any fun. He never even takes you out or buys you any presents. Why would you want to settle down?"

"For three reasons," I went on. "First, I love him. Second, we want to, and," even more quietly, "I'm pregnant."

"OUT OF THE TEN KIDS, I ALWAYS KNEW YOU WOULD BE THE BAD ONE!" she yelled.

As she left the room, she turned and said, "Tomorrow is Thanksgiving. This is the only day out of the year that all the family comes. Make sure you leave the house before dinner tomorrow. I do not want you here to ruin Thanksgiving."

I was completely stunned.

Not exactly the response I was hoping for, nor was the response from Dave when I told him and suggested, "Maybe I can come to your house for Thanksgiving."

"No, that's not a good idea. Then I will have to explain to my mom why you were not with your family. I'm not ready to tell her yet."

I cried. I was shocked.

On Thanksgiving Day 1972, I walked along the avenue doing some window shopping alone. That was the first indication that he would not be there for me as a power of strength, only I was too much in love to see it.

That was when I realized how lucky I was to have this terrific job. Once I told my boss, Dot, about my pregnancy, she immediately started looking into moving me into the Dictaphone Typing Department because it paid more than a file clerk.

My cousin Audrey had been in her friend's wedding in September. After hearing that Dave and I were planning on getting married, she offered to lend us all the dresses from the bridal party, including the bridal gown of her friend who just happened to wear the same size as me. At that time, I had two best friends, Margaret and Peggy. It was hard to decide who would be my maid of honor, but the decision was made for me, by who fit into which dress, and we all laughed about the fact that I did not have to choose.

Between the fact of having the dresses and having my job give me a promotion so I could make more money on January 13, 1973, we had a beautiful and traditional church wedding with hopes that I would please my mom, who always talked about seeing one of her daughters have a church wedding. I think this was the thing that finally made her come around.

Since my mon's drinking was out of control, the support I received from my friends at work became even more important to me. They threw me a beautiful bridal shower, attended my wedding, and then a few months later, also threw a baby shower. What great friends. I don't know how I would have gotten through without their support. New Jersey Machine was not just a job; it was my life.

It did not take long for me to realize that MOM WAS RIGHT. Dave turned out to be a horrible husband, always taking off from work for no reason, going out with his friends till all hours of the night, and then while I was seven months pregnant, the physical abuse started. He came home with friends from work wanting me to make breakfast for them after working the night shift at the post office. What he didn't think of was that I had nothing in the house to make for breakfast. I was waiting on his paycheck to go grocery shopping. So when he came home, two friends in tow, I asked to speak with him in the bedroom so I could quietly tell him I had nothing to feed his friends. He went wild. He left with them to eat at the diner after cashing his check at the bank, then went to a local bar and didn't show back home until 2:00 p.m. When he came home, I was ironing my clothes, and he went crazy, picking up the iron and throwing it across the room, yelling that I embarrassed him in front of his friends, then he started to hit me across the head. The landlady came running up the stairs, and he said he accidently knocked over the ironing board and everything was fine.

I was in complete shock. Never in all these years of dating had I ever seen this side of him.

After confiding in my friend Kathy from work about the incident, she immediately opened up her home to me. And then gave me such great advice.

She said, "Even though everyone is going to tell you that you have to leave Dave, don't do it until you yourself is ready." She said, "I can't explain it, but you will know when you are ready. And when you leave, you will leave for good, assured in the fact that you did the right thing."

As time went on, the abusive incidents increased, and people would be suspicious, and when I confided in someone, the advice would always be the same, "Leave him," but always Kathy's words would play in my head.

On July 8, my beautiful baby girl Claudette was born. Dave was so excited when I first went into labor; he drove so slow getting to the hospital that we were pulled over by the police. When they found out I was in labor, they gave us an escort. It was back in the day that fathers were not in the delivery room, but at least, I was hoping he would have waited in the waiting room until she was born, but he didn't. He went to the bar. He was so drunk his friend Mikey drove him home and was the one who answered the phone when the hospital called to say the baby was born at 4:47 a.m.

Dave did not come to the hospital until after twelve the next day—no flowers or anything, saying he did not have any money for flowers. I was in the hospital for three days. On Wednesday morning, I was supposed to be discharged with the baby at eleven; once again, he did not show. I had to call my mom, who came to pick me up, and we needed to walk to her house, which was a block away from the hospital. Dave showed up at her house after showing up at the hospital at 3:00 p.m., saying he just woke up and they told him I was released to my mom. She was furious and did not want me to go home with him, but I did. For a couple of months, he tried to be a good husband and father, changing her and feeding her and helping with the housework, but when she was five months old, the physical abuse started up again.

There was no way I could tell my mom about it. That was when my friends from work Kathy and Penny helped me. Penny, who became Claudette's godmother, would often stop at the house and hang out sometime late in the day waiting for him to go to work before leaving. Financially, things were so bad Dave would leave for work as a graveyard shift worker at the post office but would go to the bar instead and come home about 3:00 a.m., saying they got out early because there was no work. Many times, he would get suspended from work for being absent too much, until finally, he lost his job completely. Kathy and Penny would often help with formula and diapers while I was on maternity leave. When I was back at work, they never let me pay them back.

My mom's drinking took its toll, and she became hospitalized for eight months with cirrhosis of the liver before she passed away in August of 74. My friends from work were my rock through that as well. She died never knowing how right she was about Dave.

Finally, in April, when I went back to work, all of my work friends were so supportive. Not only did I get my job back after my maternity leave, but I was given another job as addressograph operator to give me a bigger salary. My boss was always looking out for her workers. Being a single mother herself, I guess she had compassion for her workers who were struggling.

Once I was back at work and started to feel a little more in control, I had Claudette in nursery school and had steady pay checks coming. I started to think of leaving Dave or, at least, asking him to leave, then I found out I was pregnant. No way could I leave with a toddler and a new baby. I guess I will have to make the best of it and hope everything would work out.

Dave came home one day screaming and yelling that the house was not clean and I better clean it. The next day I spent the whole day cleaning and shampooing the rug, and I moved the console TV to make sure he would see how clean everything was.

The following week, I went for my doctor's checkup, and he discovered the baby was not growing; after two more visits, it was determined the baby and afterbirth had disconnected and therefore the baby would probably miscarry. That was in June. Day after day,

I continued to go to work and take care of Claudette and the house waiting for something to happen. It was a little difficult since one of the girls in the office was pregnant and I knew my baby was not alive. Unfortunately, for me the baby did not miscarry normally, and I had to have surgery to remove it. It was August 27. The surgery caused me to have to be out of work for a while, and Dave's drinking increased, as well as the insults and abuse. His insults would include things like, what kind of a woman was I, I couldn't even keep the baby alive, his other friends' wives were able to have more than one baby, why couldn't I?

Finally, on April 13, 1977, Dave called home to say to have his dinner ready at six because he was going to play baseball at seven then go to work after that. I made steak, french fries, and string beans; everything was piping hot by six. Dave did not show up until eleven; they won the baseball game then went to the bar to celebrate so he could not go to work, but he was hungry and wanted to eat. This was long before microwaves, so when I reheated the food, of course the steak was like rubber, and the fries needed to be put back into the grease again to get hot. He was tired of waiting and grabbed my dress, ripping it as he pushed me out of the way, saying he would cook himself. The cups were in his way, so he threw them across the room, causing Claudette to wake up, running to me scared. After breaking the ketchup bottle by dropping it on the floor, he picked it up and started to hit me over the head. He was screaming and yelling about what a bad wife and mother I was and I couldn't cook or keep the baby alive or keep the house clean and that no one liked me and he was embarrassed I was his wife. Claudette stood next to me crying. When he got so mad, he reached for the greasy pot, and it was hot, so he threw it. The grease hit the floor just inches from where she was standing. As I watched the linoleum bubble before my eyes, Kathy's words came in my ears. "*YOU WILL KNOW WHEN YOU ARE READY TO LEAVE.*"

So after I got Claudette back to bed and cleaned up the mess in the kitchen trying desperately not to cut my fingers because my hands were shaking so much, I tiptoed into the bedroom where he was sleeping, at least I thought he was, but no. Lying wide awake, he wanted to apologize, and what better way than by having sex. He even joked that he put my shoes in his pillowcase just in case I thought about leaving. After telling him I accepted his apology and pretending that I enjoyed our lovemaking, I lay there, and once his breathing was level, I was convinced he was asleep. I was ready.

Afraid of making noise by opening drawers, I pulled my ripped dress covered in blood and ketchup with pieces of glass mixed in back on and lifted Claudette out of her bed. I put my hands over her mouth so she wouldn't make a sound. Then I walked barefoot to my brother Richard's house. I knew right then and there that Kathy was right. I knew for sure I was leaving for good. I filed for divorce the very next day.

Once again, my job came through for me when they gave me two weeks off (paid), so when Dave repeatedly showed up at my job, they told him they had to let me go and I no longer worked there. Little did he know I spent those two weeks at Charlie and Barbara's house, his brother and sister-in law, somewhere he never thought to look for me and Claudette. One of the salesmen from my job drove me to Charlie's house who lived out of town.

By the time I returned to town, Dave had been served with divorce papers and a restraining order, which helped at least temporarily.

I guess thirteen really did turn out to be my lucky number; it was my thirteenth interview that I got this awesome job, then got married on the thirteenth, which was not all bad, then my divorce was finalized on April 13, 1978.

As I started my life over as a single mom, my work friends once again were there for me, making sure Claudette had what she needed. And when her nursery school closed for two weeks, my boss had it okayed that she come to work with me. Eileen, one of the secretaries, purchased her very own Micky Mouse desk.

To help me out financially very often, the salesmen and men working in the shop would give me rides up to the nursery school so I could save the bus fare. I was so fortunate and appreciative for their help and support I worked extra hard to do a great job.

1978

Claudette was now in kindergarten, and Dave was pretty much an absentee father, except for on the few occasions when he had a girlfriend who he wanted to show her off to. As she grew, so did our financial needs. She needed eye glasses, which was not covered under my insurance, and because she was attending Catholic school, there were uniforms and book bills and, of course, Girl Scouts and soccer and half-day kindergarten rather than full day at the nursery school. The need for half-day babysitter was there. What wasn't there was the child support that was court-ordered from Dave. So although I was happy at my job, the need to look for a higher-paying job was present. I had learned shorthand but barely passed it in high school, so I purchased a shorthand book and refreshed my skills so I could apply for a secretarial position, and as luck would have it, I found a terrific job closer to home, paying more money as a secretary to five salesmen in a small business called PKP Inc. All the other workers were older women whose children were already grown, and I was the only one with a young child.

Claudette became everyone's little mascot. When her school was closed and I couldn't find a babysitter, my boss would allow me to bring her to work, which really helped me out. I didn't know how lucky I was to have found another great job with brand-new work friends.

During this time in my life, I started to miss having a partner to share my life with. I had been content to stay pretty much at home and be just a mom up to that point, but now she was older and was agreeable to spend the evening with a babysitter, so I could go out. Money was so tight that very often my girlfriend Fran and I would take turns babysitting for each other. I would bring Claudette to her house, or she would bring her kids to my house, which also freed up our homes if we chose to have overnight guest, which wasn't such a bad arrangement, so no money would have to change hands, and also Claudette would be happy to have someone to play with while I was out. It was a win/win situation.

Working in a job where there were available men and some not so available, I'm ashamed to say, dates were not too hard to come by. I was in my midtwenties, about 112 pounds, and not so bad looking, so male attention was definitely evident. Up until this point in my life, Dave was my one and only, and my sex life with him was quite active, which for the most part, thanks to my mom's advice, I enjoyed. While eight months pregnant, I went to a play with friends from work. Knowing Dave would be working overnight, I decided to spend the night at my mom's house, but when I got there, no one was home. Being very aware of my mom's habits, I walked down to the neighborhood bar, and sure enough, she was there, not exactly sober. I ordered a soda and sat with her for a while. That was when she decided to have *the talk* with me.

"Well," she said, "I guess it's a little too late for me to tell you about the birds and bees. You already figured it out."

I sat there quite embarrassed and not sure what to expect, then she blurred out, "The one thing you should know is this: You should not get into the bed with him unless you want, and don't get out until you're finished, and I don't mean he's satisfied, I mean you. It is all right for you to enjoy sex. It's not just for men to enjoy."

Wow, I thought, *this definitely is not what I was expecting. It is like getting permission from my mother to enjoy sex.* And it proved to serve me well throughout my life. Thanks, Mom.

Although I will not deny an occasional one-night stand, for which I was never comfortable, I did start to date when Claudette was about five. I met a very nice divorced man with two older children whose name was Dan. He was fifteen years older than me, but we got along great. He adored Claudette and was very attentive to me. I met him at work; he was a client and pretty well respected by my coworkers. The more serious we got, the more scared I got. He introduced me to his children, and he met my brothers and sisters.

It was about this time he told me he had gotten a vasectomy and would not be having more children. That was a deal breaker for me. I so wanted more children and was not ready to give up the dream. As time went on, I started to find fault with almost everything he did and soon ended the relationship, which was difficult because I still had to see him occasionally when he came into the job.

As time went on, I started to advance at the job and soon became the secretary to the president of the company, whose family lived in another state. It didn't take long before my secretarial skills turned into other skills. My boss treated me and Claudette like we were his own family, and eventually my dating was exclusive with just him. He was with us during the week and his real family during the weekend. I knew it was wrong, but when someone in a high position like president of a company and twice your age showered you with so many gifts and attention, it was hard to do the right thing. The age difference between me and him was the same between Monica Lewinsky and President Clinton. I could understand how she felt. You knew it was wrong, but you did it anyway.

Each time I introduced him to my family and friends, I would say he was divorced. Eventually when I would attend a wedding or weekend event, always with an excuse that he was away on business or his kid's birthday or something, I was sure everyone knew the truth but never confronted me. In addition to the royal treatment we received from the president, we also were treated well by the other salesmen at work, but not for the same reasons. Just genuinely nice guys. Claudette was growing quickly, and very often around the holidays, my coworkers would purchase Christmas gifts for her. Very often the gifts would be nicely wrapped and signed by their wife. It seemed that they appreciated how hard I worked and realized how difficult it was to raise a child with one income. Of course, they were not aware of my relationship with the boss. We were extremely careful to be discrete. Whenever his wife would call or visit, I would always be overly friendly so as not to make anyone suspicious.

The economy in the '70s was not very good, and at one point, everyone had been cut to a four-day workweek instead of laying anyone off. This, of course, was quite a hardship for me. Losing one day's pay really hurt, as I was living paycheck to paycheck. On the weeks when the book bill was due at Claudette's school or there was some other unexpected financial burden, I would walk to work, which was approximately twenty blocks away. I never told anyone at work my problems, but I think they knew because one day I went into to work and was told that I could work my regular five days. Apparently, a couple of the men decided they would give up an extra day each month so I could work five days. I couldn't believe that they would do that for me—and expected nothing in return. On another occasion, I was at work and my neighbor called to say she saw two men coming out of my house carrying my TV and she called the police. By the time they got there, the robbers were gone. They had stolen my typewriter, $55 in cash, which I was saving for Claudette's new glasses, and a few smaller items, like my wedding rings and Claudette's cross she got for her communion. And of course, the lock was broken.

One of the salesmen, Al, drove me home. It was horrible. The creeps threw things all over the house and broke the doll carriage she had gotten for Christmas. My first thought was that if they didn't take the money, I would use it to call the locksmith, but of course they did.

Claudette and I stayed at a friend's that night, and when I went to work the next morning, there was an envelope on my desk, no signature, but with more than enough cash to pay for a locksmith and a note that said, "Buy Claudette a new doll carriage."

It turned out one of the other women told me Al told everyone what had happened and they all took up a collection. I was so appreciative, and all they said was, "Just keep doing a good job with raising your daughter and working hard, and things will always work out." Such a true statement.

During the time I was working at PKP, Dave would try to come back into our lives. As much as it was tempting putting the family back together and having Claudette have her father again, I must say the encouragement I received from the men I worked with was priceless. These men were successful businessmen with families of their own who wanted nothing from me, only to see me happy, and they would tell me over and over how I deserved to be treated well and I should not accept a man who hurt me, whether it be physically or mentally. I started to think they were right, and it also made me realize how wrong I was to date a married man, even if he did treat me well. I deserved a man who was all mine. I also felt guilty to have been the other woman. I realized how uncomfortable it would be to work there after I left the personal relationship with my boss.

When I told him about my plan to end our personal relationship, we both agreed it would be uncomfortable for me to continue working there, so I started to look for a job elsewhere. I got a wonderful reference from the salesmen that I put down as references and got the first job I applied for working at a lawyer's office. Because I would not be working too far away, I very often had lunch with a few of my coworkers, completely platonic friendships. Those are the best kind, where you can be completely honest and know they have your best interest at heart.

It's so funny how God puts people in your life and you don't realize the impact they have until years later. There was this one salesman I worked with named Al. He loved his wife so much and was such a family guy that I would always think when I did meet someone who would be a husband to me, I hoped he was just like Al. I did not think of him romantically. I just loved how he loved his wife and let it show. I felt she was the luckiest woman in the world to have him thinking about her like that. He also would say things like, "Time is going to pass whether you do something good with the time or not, so you might as well."

Even though he had a great job, he went back to school at nights to get a degree. He would often ask me if I could be anything in the world, what would it be. I told him I always wanted to be a court reporter but my mother could not afford to pay for the school, so I couldn't go.

He would say, "So go now."

I had been out of high school ten years at that point and never even thought about going back, but he got me thinking. I started to talk about it all the time, never really knowing how I would be able to do it, but then one day at a family party, my nephew Steve's graduation, my brother John heard me going on and on about wanting to go to school.

He had said, "Hey, Bernice, if you are serious, I will help you go back to school financially, but you have to take it serious and not waste my money."

"Yes, of course, I would love to be a court reporter."

Well, the very next day, I pulled out my trusty manual typewriter since the electric typewriter had been stolen and sent a letter to Mr. Fix-It in the *Jersey Journal* asking for information on court reporting schools in the area.

On September 7, 1981, I started American Business Academy Court Reporting school in Hackensack, New Jersey, twice a week, Monday and Thursday evenings, and was in my glory. I went every Monday and Thursday 6:00 to 9:30 p.m. and studied like crazy to keep up until the school discontinued their evening classes due to lack of students enrolled in the evenings. When I started, there were thirty-seven students, but gradually, we were down to half that because the course was so hard students were dropping out. It took almost a year for me to find another court reporting school, but in January of '83, I started Century Institute of Court Reporting, also in Hackensack.

Just over a year of attending Century, once again, my academic career came to a halt when this school, due to the large number of students dropping out because the course was so hard, also discontinued their evening classes.

Working in a lawyer's office only made me more determined to become a court reporter. It was so cool to see the court reporters come in for depositions I couldn't get enough of asking questions of them.

Between working full-time and being a mom, I was always quite busy, but I really did think a lot about a serious boyfriend; the guy I had been casually dating had so much baggage. He and his ex-wife were still so friendly that he often babysat for their four children in her home. You can imagine how uncomfortable it was for me when he would invite us to his ex-wife's house for dinner.

"Oh, it is so much better for the kids if they see everyone getting along," he would say.

I would often think back to what Al used to say. "You deserve a guy who treats you special, who respects you and who is yours alone."

Somehow, I thought Bill would always be attached to his ex and I would never be number one. Although I did continue dating Bill, I was sure it was not going last.

One evening after a long day at work and then a doctor's visit afterward, I was looking forward to a quiet evening at home. Claudette was at a sleepover at her friend's house. As I was leaving the doctor's office, my friend showed up and begged me to go with her for a drink. She needed someone to talk to. I went to a club with my friend Fran to console her after she had one of the many fights with her on-again, off-again useless boyfriend Harry. We walked into Joey G's, which was completely empty with the exception of one guy sitting in the corner. Seeing he was not bad looking and was by himself, my thought was to get Fran interested in him and I could leave. I heard him ask for his check from the bartender when he caught me looking over at him. Then he walked over to the jukebox and put some music on.

After a few moments, he came over and said hello and asked if I wanted to dance. What I really wanted was to leave and have him dance with Fran, but I said yes anyway. Then he asked if he could join us. In my mind, I thought I could get them two talking and then quietly leave, but it didn't take me long to change my mind. It turned out Pete was a great guy and very good-looking. He talked about his daughter and how she was handicapped and he was a single dad, and then he talked about his other two children, who were from his second wife and that he had custody of them as well while he was in the process of getting a divorce, and before long, I was head over heels in love. He was such a gentleman that he danced with both Fran and me, and before long, she was the one who wanted to leave instead of me.

We laughed when we heard the bartender call "Last call" because we were having such a good time we did not realize how late it was. As Fran and I prepared to leave, I was saddened that he did not ask for my number as he walked us to Fran's car. Early in our conversation, I mentioned I had a boyfriend named Bill.

When Fran and I were just about to pull out of the parking lot, Pete's truck pulled next to her car, and he handed me his number and said, "I don't hone in another man's lady, but here is my number in case you ever break up."

That was when I realized I finally met a man who seemed to want to treat me well. Here was a real gentleman. I handed him my number and said I was sure Bill and I would be through. By the time Fran dropped me off, my home phone was already ringing. We wound up talking so long my alarm went off and I went to work with absolutely no sleep.

The next day I met with Bill and told him I was not going to see him anymore. Unfortunately, that did not go over well. He constantly called and showed up at my job, promising me a brighter future if I would change my mind. It is so funny how someone only appreciates you when the relationship is about to end. Previously, Bill would call me Ralph as a joke because he teased that Bernice was such a formal name like Ralph is a formal men's name. One night when I came home from a date with Pete, we pulled up to my house, and on the porch was a big banner saying, "Love you, Ralph. Want you back."

I was so appalled. Pete, on the other hand, was confused. Why would someone leave a message for Ralph on my porch.

"I'm Ralph," I said, which only made him more confused, wondering what he was getting himself into.

The following day, a car was parked in front of my job with a similar message written on a cloth. While I was frantically trying to remove the sign, my boss came by and said, "Why are you taking that sign off the car?"

I said, "Because I'm Ralph."

Needless to say, I should have just left it alone. No one would have thought anything of it.

What a small world this is because one evening afterward, Pete and I went to a bar where he was competing in a pool tournament, and Bill's ex-wife just happened to be there. Turned out Pete knew her. It was not like we lived in a small town where everyone usually knew one another. We lived in Jersey City, the second largest city in New Jersey.

At first, I would reflect back on what Al used to say about how I deserved a guy who would be mine alone and I would think, *Wow, Pete really loves me and treats me so well*, making me feel so important. But it didn't take long before the problems started. Claudette, by this time, was twelve years old, and his daughter Sammy was fifteen, and then there was Marcy, who was four, and his son Jackie, who was nineteen months old. I was so blinded by my love for him that I tried to be a superwoman, trying to keep everyone happy.

After dating for one year and being so in love, I immediately said yes when Pete suggested we move in together. We tried so hard to make everyone comfortable with the move. Both daughters had dogs, so we decided rather than allow one to keep their dog and knowing it was too hard to keep both dogs, we had them both give up their dogs, which was good because dogs were not allowed in our new home. We took tape measures to all apartments so we could make sure that both girls' rooms would be the same size. The only apartment that fit our needs was in North Bergen, which was a big problem since we lived in Jersey City.

So we made a clean break from the city and moved to a completely neutral town. We rented the apartment in North Bergen, allowing both girls to finish the year in their respective schools since we moved in March. Claudette was entering eighth grade and begged to be able to graduate with her friends, which meant a year of extra expense for bus fare, but in my efforts to make everyone happy, I agreed.

For the next couple of years, things were good between me and Pete, but problems between Pete and Claudette and Sammy and me were not so great. That was when we began to have the "your daughter, my daughter" fights. "Sammy would eat in her room," or "Claudette would not do the dishes." "Sammy failed her subjects in school," and "Claudette would stay out too late with her friends" were common arguments in the household. The girls were so different we would try to force a friendship in them by occasionally going out to dinner just us four or camping trips with just them, but it never really worked. After a while, we started to allow them to each bring a friend with them when we would go on vacation just to keep the peace.

Pete's ex-wife Brooke got married around this time, and Pete agreed to give her back custody of the kids. At first, everything was going well. We would visit with them every other weekend and one day during the week. Then she started to cause problems about the kids spending time at our home. Since Pete and I were not married, she tried to make that an issue, requesting that I leave the home whenever the children would stay over, even though she lived with Pete before they got married when Sammy was little. She had a new husband who wanted the children to be adopted by him, so she kept trying to accuse us of things that would cause the court to end Pete's parental rights. Funny, she never wanted to end the child support though.

Many frivolous court appearances brought up by her caused so many arguments with us and also legal fees. She would accuse us of not taking care of the kids when they would visit even though they would love to be with us. On one occasion, Marcy, who was four at the time, would say things like, "My mommy said you're bad because you sleep with my daddy and you're not married."

Other times, as the kids got older, when Marcy and Jackie were in school, their mom would purposely tell us the wrong time for a teacher's conference or cheerleading or football game, knowing we had to travel over an hour to get there, then tell the kids, "See, if Daddy really cared, he would have been here."

We had visitation rights every other weekend and four weeks during the summer, which was nice for Pete, but if truth be known, when the kids were with us, it was me, not him, who did all the work. Also, my two weeks' vacation from work was usually when his kids visited, and his ex-wife took her two weeks' vacation while we had the kids; it wasn't that nice.

When Pete and I decided to get married, we had to keep it a secret from the kids, even though they were in the wedding because we were afraid their mom keep the kids home that day on spite.

For the Love of Pete

Never was there a doubt that I loved Pete with all my heart, and for the most part, I could say we did have a great marriage, considering all the extra stressors we always dealt with.

When we first got together, we both had pretty good jobs, and then he got laid off when AT&T divested and his job was eliminated. He got a pretty good severance pay and then sold the home he owned, and for a few years, we had been able to keep up with the finances of everyday life. He was very generous with his money, and neither he nor I were ever careful with money, and it would come to haunt us throughout our marriage.

At the time Pete was laid off, I had a job working for Jersey City Law Department, and with his severance pay and my income, we pretty much were taking it easy, going on vacations with the kids and buying camping equipment and often eating out instead of cooking at home, and before you know it, the money was almost all gone. Neither one of our faults, but both of us careless.

It took awhile for him to find a job, and unfortunately, not having other skills outside of AT&T, it was difficult finding just the right job making a decent salary, but with the help of Unemployment, he was given the opportunity to be part of a program where they worked along with corporations to train people on unemployment where the companies paid half and the Unemployment paid half of the salary.

It served Pete well, and he learned a new trade installing telephone systems in businesses, which he thoroughly enjoyed and was very good at it, and he received praise from his job numerous times.

Within the next couple of years, we got married and had a beautiful baby. Life was definitely good.

While on a camping trip up to Vernon, we started talking about how nice it would be to live in the mountains. Just a pipe dream, but then I got laid off from my job, and we took it as a sign that the time was right for such a big move.

My daughter Claudette had just graduated high school and was off to college, and Sammy was excited about the move. Pete was okay with an hour commute, so we made the move and rented a big house that cost less in rent than our five-room apartment did in North Bergen.

Within the next couple of months, Pete's job ended because the company got sold. Now I was already on unemployment, and he was now without a job with absolutely no savings. I was lucky to find a job as a waitress at a resort, and we were able to make ends meet.

It was at this time that Pete started to talk about starting his own business. He was good at his job and had a lot of people already willing to have him become their phone guy for their business, so he took a couple of classes with the SEP Program, helping him to get started with a small business. He used all the initials of the kids' names and started his own business, NJACS, and registered with the State of New Jersey.

At first, it was great, and he was able to make connections with larger interconnect companies that would hire him for their extra workload.

With his business doing well and me working at the resort, we also were able to purchase a home, a handyman special, which was fine because Pete was so handy. We refinanced right after the closing to put in new windows and doors and fix the floors, all the work done by Pete, saving lot of money from having to hire a professional, but the work was done just as well by him.

During the time he was doing well in his business, I had an opportunity to go back to school to become a court reporter, which was quite an exciting thing since I had attempted going to school three previous times and this was the first time I would be able to go in the day and, hopefully, complete the course once and for all.

When I finished school and got a job working in my field, his business started to get really slow. The economy had taken a slide, and many of the interconnect companies that would hire him for their extra work had stopped calling, instead giving the work to their regular workers because of slow time period. Also, our inability to invest in his business by him learning the new digital phone systems that were new to the field, gradually, his business was barely holding on.

At this time, we decided to refinance again because our stairs needed replacing in the front of the house. Instead of just fixing the stairs, we decided to put on a front porch we lived right across from the lake, and we felt it was a good investment, but when we first started to find a contractor, we were giving prices between $8,000 and $10,000. Unable to afford those estimates, Pete researched at the library how to install a front porch. He went to the town, got all the permits, and rented a backhoe, and within eight days, we had a beautiful new porch, which was my favorite part of the house, and also a higher mortgage payment to go along with the new porch. By this time, Pete was fifty-seven years old, and as his business hung on by a thread, he was having no luck finding a job. After going on interviews, he would come home feeling pretty confident that he got the job, only to get a call or letter saying they went with another candidate. Guess it made more sense to hire a younger person to do the job. So he was too young for Social Security but too old to get a job? A vicious cycle.

Because Pete had more time on his hands because of his inability to find a job, he started to work on his old cars. He was an antique car enthusiast, and had four antique cars, two he had had since before I met him, a 1962 Chevy truck and a 1961 Chevy Impala, his pride and joy. And two cars that were left to him from a family friend when she passed away, 1955 Buick and 1969 Cadillac.

It was not feasible to work on these cars in the driveway, so he and his friend rented a garage to work on the cars. He always said they were an investment, and if things got really bad financially, we would be able to sell them. This was his reasoning to spend the monthly rental fee for the garage to house the cars.

By this time, my job was terrific. I was a CART Provider for Bergen County Special Services, working in Midland Park School system, and was lucky enough have a skill that was in great demand. After a few years of working at the school, I was approached about providing CART at Bergen County Community College for students with hearing loss during the evenings classes and soon also was lucky enough to get work at Kean College, as well as Montclair.

Within a few months, I decided to start my own business called See What They're Saying, which was registered in New Jersey and New York.

I started to work at the college in the evenings and started getting request to provide CART Services in New York City for meetings working with adults with hearing loss; many times the meetings were held in the evenings and on Saturdays. But I also continued to work full-time at Midland Park School.

As time went on, I started to work more and more, and our financial situation improved.

I was starting to feel a resentment or kind of jealously especially where the kids were concerned. Pete would very often tell me how exciting it was that Nadine assisted in making the winning goal at her soccer game or that Jackie ran the ball sixty-five yards at his football game. In addition to the resentment, I guess you can say I was also jealous about his relationship with the kids. Intellectually, I knew it was not entirely his fault he couldn't find a job. After all, who wants to hire a fifty-seven-year-old guy when there are so many young guys out of work, but that did not stop me from wanting to cut back on working so much and be able to attend the sports games of the kids. I was starting to feel like an absentee parent. Nadine let me know that Pete's french braid was tighter than the ones I did. The only time it seemed that I spent any time with her was when I taught her CCD class and maybe on Sundays.

In summer of 2006, my side business was pretty good, and between what I made there and my regular income, things financially was pretty good.

Then Pete said why not add on a garage onto the house. We could save the rental we were paying for the garage, and it would add the investment on the house, so once again, we refinanced to put on the garage. Pete was so handy that we just paid for the foundation and the frame, and he finished the rest of the garage himself. He put in the lighting and walls and siding, as well as the roof, saving us a ton of money. He did a great job, and we even celebrated by having a garage christening party.

When the summer was over and I went back to work at the school and also was anticipating getting my college classes back, my college student advised me that she was going to be taking online classes, so therefore, she did not need my services for that semester.

Between the higher mortgage payment and the loss of income from these college classes, things started to go from bad to worse. I was now able to see more high school games with the kids, but the stress of not having enough money to pay the bills caused a great amount of stress between us.

So now was the time for Pete to prove that the cars we had been hauling around forever would actually be the investment he promised.

His love for old cars overshadowed his common sense one afternoon in late October.

With our financial situation getting pretty bad because of bad decisions on both our parts, we talked about the fact he used to always say we had these antique cars as an investment we could always fall back on if we needed to.

Well, now certainly was the time to fall back on that sentiment. He had the 1951 Chevy up for sale which he purchased a year prior with the intent of restoring and selling, and a guy came to look at it. I was so excited I stood on the porch and listened to the guy and him talking about the car.

Pete was asking $4,200 for it. The guy really wanted it and said that he could give him $3,800 in cash, more than what we needed to pay all the bills up to day. He had the tow truck right there at the end of the driveway and was ready to make the deal. I was so excited I went into the house and was waiting for them to make the deal.

This was going to make our situation so much better, and hopefully, we would learn from our poor decisions and be more careful with money. A couple of minutes went by, I went in and listened by the bedroom window, and I heard the guy say to Pete, "Well, I'm sorry we can't make a deal. I got $3,800 here in cash, and the truck is ready. Are you sure you won't change your mind?"

And Pete said, "No, man, we both know it is worth $4,200."

They shook hands, and I thought I was going to die.

I was shaking with rage and could barely breathe. The bills were through the roof, and I was already working as many hours as I could. What happened to "These cars are an investment"? What happened to "We can always fall back on the cars—we will sell them when we need to"? I started to yell at him when he came in.

And he said, "You don't know anything about cars. This guy was trying to rip me off. That car is worth more than $3,800, and he knows it. Watch, he'll be back."

Today, January 12, 2018, the car is still in the driveway, and I'm still waiting for him to come back.

I guess he realized his decision to not sell the car was really crazy, so then he started to actively look for a job—any job, just something to make peace with me. He found a driver job working delivering mulch, and he worked there until age sixty-two, when he was able to retire.

It seemed we had a really strong relationship to survive this roller-coaster ride with so many ups and downs.

My business started to improve, and in addition to my full-time job, I was now working three nights a week, as well as every other Saturday, for a student in college going for his master's degree. Lucky for me, this job was for eighteen months—exhausting, yes, but the money was great, which surely came in handy.

Now with the kids grown, we had a lot more expenses. I guess the saying "Small children, small problems. Big kids, big problems" also relates to finances. Between braces, car insurance, college, and wedding expenses, we never could quite catch up no matter how much I worked.

When Pete retired, he was very happy. After all, his social security was steady money, contributing toward the bills now, so he was good.

The thing about Pete that is both good and also frustrating is that he takes friendship very seriously. He is very talented when it comes to home repairs. Very often he would help out our friends and family doing handyman work for them when needed, such as installing a toilet or sink, and for one neighbor, he installed all new screens in their screen house, repaired a deck on another friend's mobile home, and everyone raved about what great work he did, and because he wasn't working, he had a lot of time to get the work done in a timely fashion. So what's the problem?

Well, Pete did not feel comfortable taking money from his friends, so whenever they tried to pay him, his reply would always be, "Nah, I don't make money off the backs of my friends."

What a nice guy, but this did nothing to help with our finances.

On a few occasions, we would argue about it, and I would tell him it was a *win/win* situation for all they could get quality work done at a discount price from someone they could trust and we could get a couple of dollars to help out with growing pile of bills.

With regard to Pete, my emotions were always all over the place. He was by no means lazy and always helped with the housework. One day after working a fourteen-hour day, I got home at 11:00 p.m. and was so tired all I could think of was to crash in bed and pass out. I quickly sent my student his notes and headed for the bedroom. When I put on the light, I lost it. There were three piles of folded clothes on the bed. I started to scream while throwing the clothes on the floor, stating how tired I was and did not want to put the clothes away. Needless to say, this caused a huge argument, and then I was too angry to even sleep.

The next day at lunch, I was telling my coworkers about the clothes on the bed, expecting sympathy from them. What I did not expect was to have gotten hit in the head with a piece of aluminum foil, playfully thrown by my friend Vicky.

She said, "He sorted the clothes. He washed the clothes and folded the clothes, and you have the nerve to complain because he did not put them away. My husband does not even know where our washer is."

Then my friend Linda chimed in and said, "I'm with Vicky. I was just looking at your lunch. Isn't that breaded pork chops and potatoes and broccoli? Did you go to a restaurant for your lunch?"

"No," I said. "Pete made it for dinner for him and the kids last night and made extra."

Then she said, "If my husband had to feed the kids, it would have been to order a pizza."

Wow, I was expecting them to understand how angry I was to have the clothes on the bed, and all the sympathies were for Pete, not me.

I started to think about what they said for the rest of the day, remembering how just recently a neighbor mentioned how nice our house looked and had great curb appeal. I also was trying to remember the last time I had actually done the wash, or for that matter, any house cleaning at all. I suddenly started looking at our situation differently. They were right. I was lucky. Maybe Pete was not working outside the house, but he kept our house in great shape, both inside and out, and it was true that my skill afforded me the opportunity to make more money, so it made us a team.

Pete was so helpful to me in my business also. Knowing how I hated to drive in New York City, we would very often drive me so I wouldn't be stressed out from the trip, which I so appreciated.

He also drove me to jobs that I had in Boston, as well as Philadelphia, and hung out for hours waiting for me to complete these jobs. So I guess what he lacked in his willingness to sell the cars to make extra money or get another part-time job after his retirement made up for it.

Together we have raised five children, experienced many celebrations with our children, became grandparents to three beautiful grandchildren, had a fire in our home, was displaced for ninety-nine days where we had to stay in a hotel before purchasing a home together, helped each other through medical issues, and survived the tragedy of losing a daughter at the tender age of forty-five, and I can honestly say there is no one in this entire world I would have rather gone through this life with.

Superwoman I Am Not

When I first became a mom at the age of nineteen, my daughter became my first priority, and in my heart, I just thought a day would never come when I would have to make a decision to upset her by not being there to support each and every event in her life, but life does get in the way of a mom's wish to always be there.

When my daughter was three years old, her dad and I divorced, and although for the most part, he was an absentee dad, except for the few occasions when he had a girlfriend, then it was cool for him to show her off. When Claudette was six, it just so happened Christmas Day landed on Dave's visitation day. I tried numerous times to get him to change weekends with me because I just could not stand the idea of not being with my daughter on Christmas morning, but he wouldn't budge, so my only thought was to invite him and his girl-friend to breakfast on Christmas morning so at least I would be able to enjoy her opening up her gifts, even if it was quite uncomfortable to have to serve Dave and his girlfriend breakfast as if they were sitting in a restaurant. They brought her a beautiful rabbit's fur coat, as well as clothes and a doll and necklace. She opened their gifts first, then went on to open her gifts from Santa as we three adults looked on. When she finished opening her gifts and was so excited because she got the gifts she so wished for and was on her letter to Santa, she looked up and said, "Mommy, Daddy, and Ellen got me these gifts, and Santa got me these gifts, but you did you get me, anything?"

I couldn't believe it. Dave just sat there grinning from ear to ear.

"That's because my gift is a surprise," I said as my brain was trying to decide what it could possibly be. I said, "What have you been wishing for that is not under the tree?"

Then she smiled really big and said, "Melanie just got her ears pierced. Is that my surprise?"

"You guessed it," I said even though I was not planning on getting her ears pierced until she was older. Within the next couple of minutes, Dave, Ellen, and Claudette left so she could have the rest of the day with Ellen's family.

On other occasions, Dave would show up only to make situations harder than they needed to be. When Claudette was in fourth grade, she had been in Catholic school, and I made the decision to keep my marital status to myself mainly because I truly hated the expression "broken home." I didn't want her teachers treating her differently.

Claudette got a part in the school concert where she was singing "Somewhere over the Rainbow" as a solo. I was so very proud and told just about everybody I knew. I bought flowers and sat in the audience grinning from pride, and when the performances were over, the teacher made an announcement to meet the children in the classroom. I guess word got around because I was totally shocked when leaving the auditorium, I saw Dave with a girlfriend. As I approached the classroom, I dropped my pocketbook and handed the flowers to him while I picked up my items that spilled from the pocketbook. All of a sudden Claudette came and saw her daddy and ran to him. He handed her the flowers and bent down to give her a kiss and tell her how proud he was, then her teacher came over. Dave introduced Ellen as his girlfriend to the teacher, which was quite shocking to her since she didn't know we were divorced. It was like I was invisible to Claudette as she walked hand in hand with Dave and Ellen. I never even corrected her when she thanked her daddy for the flowers, nor did he, I might add.

As she got older, Dave's presence in her life was less and less, and although I did date quite often, her life did not change until I met Pete. My love for him definitely enhanced my desire to always be there for everyone. He had custody of his fifteen-year-old daughter, who not only had no contact with her mom, and also was handicapped with cerebral palsy. Luckily, it was mild and only affected her lower extremities, but also did not get along with Pete's second wife, whom he was in the process of divorcing when we met. I so wanted to prove to Pete that I was different from his previous wives and that I was going to be there for his daughter that I inadvertently neglected my own daughter after a trip to the mall and having lunch with Sammy. I got home.

Claudette said, "Hey, Mom, I'd like to introduce myself to you. Do you remember me? I'm your daughter."

I felt so terrible I didn't even realize it. In my efforts to make sure Sammy had my mothering, Pete did nothing at all to act like a dad to Claudette. It was not long before the resentments started and we started to have "your daughter, my daughter" fights. It also became evident why Sammy and Pete's second wife did not get along; she was a master player at pitting husband against wife, no matter who the wife was. The connection between Pete and Sammy was quite tight. I'm sure Pete was overly protective of her because of her disability and the fact that she had had somewhere up to ten surgeries to help with her walking.

Another problem we had was in discipline. Now that we were all living together under one roof with two teenagers, we had to have some sort of plan. It became evident that that was going to be quite difficult should my rules for Claudette change or should Pete's rules for Sammy or lack thereof change? Claudette loved going out with her friends, and Sammy preferred staying at home and watching TV, so punishing Claudette by saying she could not watch TV or telling Sammy she could not go out wasn't going to work. So we decided that we would discipline our own daughters depending on what we thought would work. On one occasion, both daughters received their report cards. Claudette got all As with the exception of one failing grade for Spanish. On the other hand, Sammy's report card was quite the opposite. My punishment for Claudette was that she had to come home right after her job and not go out with her friends until the teacher let me know she was doing better. Pete's punishment for Sammy was nil. "Just promise me you will do better." You can imagine how well that went over.

Things were not much different when the two younger children visited. Pete was raised by a very mean and abusive stepmother and therefore was not much of a disciplinarian. Once when five-year-old Jackie used scissors to cut the Christmas tree lighting and was nearly thrown across the room from the shock, Pete's punishment was to sit on the couch, with cartoons on TV, and think about what he just did. My house rules were always challenged by Sammy. No ice cream before dinner or no eating in the bedrooms were totally ignored, and Pete never backed me up.

The only time discipline was important to Pete was when it was Claudette who broke the rules. On the very same day that Sammy took the car without permission and allowed someone who did not have a license drive it in the park, Claudette did not do the dishes. It turned out to be one of the biggest fights we ever had. Pete yelled and screamed and carried on for what seemed like forever about why the dishes were not done and how it was her job to do the dishes and how he was not going to have her ignore her responsibilities. This was the first and only time in my life that I came close to physically assaulting someone. I continued to argue with him about Sammy's decision to take the car and allowing someone without a license to drive, how we could have lost everything and been sued and how someone could have gotten hurt or die, but he was relentless about the dishes. I saw red and almost lunged at him. I'm ashamed to say at that point he must have decided it would be a good idea for him and Sammy to leave. The weather was so bad at that point, and it was snowing like crazy, so he and Sammy actually slept in the van in the driveway not sure how we managed to move on after that night.

After living together for a year and feeling that we were able to say that our blended family was going to make it on August 6, 1988, we got married other than having my brother Arthur walk me down the aisle in the Women's Club in Rutherford; we had only the four children in the wedding. Claudette was my maid of honor, and instead of a best man, Pete asked Sammy to be his best girl. Marcy was our flower girl, and Jackie was ring bearer.

This was for sure one of the happiest times of my life, and soon, we added our beautiful daughter our—Yours, Mine, and Ours.

Now we had yours, mine, and ours, and it was definitely not the warm and fuzzy life you see in the movies.

By this time Claudette was fifteen years old and was quite socia-ble always out with friends and even had a steady boyfriend. She was not at all interested in babysitting her little sister, which gave fuel to a set of the new "my daughter, your daughter" fights. Sammy was always home so, of course, was more attentive to the baby and also had more experience with babies since she already had been involved with Marcy and Jackie when they were babies. Sometimes when we would want to go out, Pete would insist that Claudette babysit even though Sammy was home. Of course, I would say she did not have to since Sammy was home anyway, then he would say, "Maybe she doesn't want to," and then I would give in and make Claudette babysit, which only added to her resentment.

In an effort to always make everyone feel equal, I tried so hard to make sure everyone had the same in terms of birthday gifts or Christmas gifts and attention. I tried to attend all of Claudette's soft-ball games or school events, mostly trying to go alone, so she would have my undivided attention, then maybe stopping for ice cream. I also tried to do the same with Marcy and Jackie when they visited so they wouldn't be jealous of the baby. I threw surprise birthday parties for each and every one of the kids.

It didn't dawn on me at first how hard this blended family was for Claudette, after all, for the first twelve years of her life. Before I met Pete, it was her and only her that had my attention. Now she not only had to share me with a new husband and three stepsiblings, but now she had to share me with a baby sister that was also my daughter.

Fifteen years difference in age does not mean there is no jeal-ousy involved.

When Nadine was two, she got a new tricycle and was so excited and was begging me to take her outside to learn how to ride it. We were only outside a few minutes when Claudette came home from school, smiling broadly. She had passed her written driving test and stopped at the motor vehicle and got it stamped so she was legal to start driving lessons.

"Hurry up, Mom," she said. "Let's go."

"But I promised Nadine I would teach her how to ride her bike," I said.

"Oh, come on."

"Okay, Nadine, we will practice tomorrow," I said.

"No, Mommy, you promised," she cried.

Here I was with both my daughters vying for my attention. How do you choose? Lucky for me, Pete got home early and was able to keep Nadine outside on her bike while I took Claudette driving.

On another occasion, I was not so lucky Claudette was in Montclair College and her sorority was involved with homecoming weekend, and she was in charge of decorating a float for the homecoming parade. She was so excited and wanted me to come. Of course, I wanted to be there and told her I wouldn't miss it. Then Nadine was told that she was going to be carrying the banner in the celebration of the new playground right before her very first-ever soccer game on exactly the same day as Claudette's homecoming at the college. The college was one hour away, so it was quite impossible to make both, and Pete didn't make it easy for me by insisting I shouldn't miss Nadine's first soccer game, claiming Claudette was old enough to understand. I stressed over it for the entire week leading up to the events. After working the midnight shift at the hotel, I came home at 7:00 a.m., made breakfast for everyone, then set the alarm clock for 10:30, still not sure what decision I was going to make. I guess God knew the decision was too hard for me to make, so he made it for me. I overslept and did not get up until 2:30 p.m., too late to attend either event. To this day, I think both Claudette and Nadine don't believe I overslept that day.

As many parents do, I often questioned myself as whether or not I was a good mom, and sometimes it is not an easy question to answer. I have gotten some examples of these answers through ways of seeing my daughters' actions. I remember one time being very upset and hurt because my daughter Nadine did not call to say "Happy Thanksgiving," nor did she answer any of my calls throughout the day while away at college. I foolishly allowed this to ruin my day. Approximately 9:30 p.m., she finally called. Of course I started the conversation loudly, letting her know how hurt I was that she did not care enough to call or why she did not answer any of my calls. After my tirade was complete, she said, "My friends and I were serving Thanksgiving dinner at the soup kitchen, and we were told not to bring our phones. That's why I didn't answer you."

Wow, my emotions were all over the place. So proud of her for volunteering.

Another time I was calling Claudette at her dorm room on a Sunday morning.

Her roommate answered, "Oh, she is at church. I will tell her you called."

I laughed it off, saying, "That is what they tell parents when they call." But sure enough, when she called me back, she said, "Yes, I was at church. Do you want me to tell you about the readings? I go every Sunday, why are you so surprised?"

I look at the wonderful women my daughters have become and see how caring they are, both professional women. I am also amazed when I see how they both have maintained friendships with friends dating back to grammar school.

I know as parents we cannot take the blame or the credit for how our children turn out; we just do the best we can and know that our decisions as they grow are made out of love and well-being of our children, even when it does not seem so to them at the time. Like I said, superwoman I am not, but not for lack of trying.

The Twin Thing

For twelve whole minutes, I was a single baby, and then I was joined by my sister Bernadette. Together we joined a family of four brothers and two sisters, and then about two years later, another brother, and then one year after that, another sister. Now we were even five boys and five girls. Being a twin is so different than just a sibling, always being compared by everyone, who walked first, who talked first, who potty trained first, and it goes on and on all through life much like that. Even though people don't think they are doing anything wrong, it just is a pain, especially if you are the one who is the underdog.

I was born first, but always, I felt I was the one playing catch-up. I remember it like it was yesterday when Bernadette and I started a new school in fifth grade. Up until that point, we had gone to a very small Catholic school where there was only one class for each grade, so we were always in each other's class, but now, we were going to a public school that was much bigger and had three different classes of each grade, and the sections were segregated according to academic level. While we stood in the hallway of the school with both our parents and the school officials, we were being introduced to our new teacher, and my mom expressed the desire to have us both in the same class because that was what we were used too, but Mrs. McVicia loudly said, "Bernice should not be assigned to my class. She should be in Miss Gargulio's class," and in her opinion, it not be fair to Bernadette if she were to have to be put in the slower class, and it sure wouldn't work for me to be in the higher-level class; I would not be able to keep up. So it was decided we would be in separate classes, and I heard loud and clear the stone was set that I was not as smart as Bernadette. That sentiment stayed with me my whole life.

There were so many occasions where it was evident that academically, we were not alike. I sometimes wonder if it was not implanted in my brain at that hallway meeting if it would have made a difference in my academic schooling.

But academics was not the only thing she had on me. Domestically speaking, she could sew and knit and crochet without ever taking lessons. As we got older, she actually made all my daughters' prom dresses. I did draw the line when my daughter asked for her to make the wedding dresses. I guess it doesn't make any sense, but I felt I didn't want to share the excitement of my daughter's wedding by making the dress, something I was not capable of doing. I didn't say it made sense, but it's the way I felt at the time.

Bernadette and I share many twin coincidences, such as buying the same coat one winter even though we lived in different towns and showing up at a niece's wedding wearing the same dress, but no coincidence that we shared could compare with the one that occurred on January 20, 1989.

She had three children, two with her first husband and one with her second husband. I had one daughter, Claudette, who was fifteen, and I was recently remarried after being divorced from my first husband for eight years. I so wanted another baby, but my husband had three from his previous marriages, and my one, making four that we had custody of. So we debated back and forth on the subject and finally agreed it would be nice to have a baby between the two of us. On May 8, 1988, I discovered I was pregnant and over the moon with happiness. After first telling our other children of the great news, my next call was to my twin. Guess what, I screamed with joy, "I'm pregnant. I can't believe it, after fifteen years, I'm finally going to have another baby. I am so very excited." I went on and on forever, then finally she said, "I was going to tell you something, but I will tell you another time."

A few days later, she said she was also pregnant but didn't want to take away from my excitement. She said she was due January 25, and my doctor had confirmed my due date as January 15. Wow, we both agreed they were going to be so close in age. What we didn't know was just how close they were going to be.

On Thursday, January 19, Bernadette called to say she was going to the hospital; her labor had started. I'm not going to say I was not jealous because I was already four days past my due date. All day long, whenever the phone rang, I was expecting to hear that she had her baby. Then on January 20 at 6:00 a.m., my labor started, still no word on Bernadette's baby. I figure her husband just forgot to call. Then at 3:17 p.m., my beautiful baby girl Nadine Erica was born. I was so thrilled and was so surprised when the nurse came into the room shortly afterward to tell me I had a phone call. I didn't even get settled in my room yet. The nurse was smiling ear to ear and connected a phone up and handed it to me.

Bernadette said, "Hey, guess what, I had a girl."

"Me too," I cried.

She announced that Alison Lee was born at three fifteen that afternoon; she went on laughing. We knew they were going to be close, but two minutes. Wow, how close can they be? Considering it takes more than two minutes to deliver, you might even say they came into the world at the same time. We refer to Nadine and Alison as *twin cousins*.

Normally, women go into the hospital to have their baby and quietly come home with not much of a buzz to the outside world, but that didn't happen for me, because of the unusual circumstance of having my daughter two minutes after my twin. We made the headlines in the *Hudson Dispatch* morning paper, "TWIN SISTERS GIVE BIRTH TWO MINUTES APART." It read, "Bernice Bonilla, from North Bergen, gave birth to her daughter two minutes after her twin sister, Bernadette..."

This was a cause for me to be a little nervous. At the time my daughter was born, I was working at Jersey City Law Department, which meant you were supposed to live in the city. We had recently moved to North Bergen, and I was seeking employment out of the city closer to home when I discovered I was pregnant. Now I was concerned that I was going to lose my job before I had a replacement job, but as luck would have it, while visiting my job to show off the baby, my boss, Mr. Fodice, after admiring the baby, kind of winked at me, saying he didn't get a chance to read the paper on January 21, which made me feel more comfortable that I was not going to lose my job, giving me enough time to find another job when I was ready.

It has been a pleasure for Bernadette and I to raise our little twin cousins together, and we both try to keep the comparisons to a minimum, knowing how much we did not like being compared so much growing up. Which I think helped form their close relationship with each other.

Mean Old Stepmother

Marcy and Jackie had gone back to live with their mom December 11, 1995, after ten months of having them living with us, which was no picnic. First, their mother didn't bother with them at all, not seeing them for ten months, but then when she visited and told them she wanted them back, they began acting like little demons. Marcy would cook bacon in the house knowing that at thirteen years old, she was not allowed to cook when no one was home. The smell of bacon permeated through the house, and still, she denied cooking. When I complained to Pete, he said to me if Marcy said she didn't cook, then she didn't. Then Jackie put a string across the room so when I stepped into his room to put away clothes so I would fall, which happened. Luckily, I did not get hurt.

His comment was, "Well, you should have made him put away his own clothes. He was probably just playing and forgot to untie it."

He never stuck up for me; he always sided with the kids even when they were disrespectful to me, and they would also tease Nadine by telling her they were playing a great game in their room but she couldn't. On another occasion, Jackie had not eaten his cheese crackers with peanut butter at lunch, so while emptying out the lunchboxes, I put them on the table.

Nadine, who was four at the time, asked for some crackers, and Jackie said, "No, they're mine from lunch."

I asked Jackie to share with Nadine. He said no and put them in the cabinet, saying he was going to save them till the morning. I explained to Jackie I could get more crackers the next day, of course. Nadine started crying; he would not budge, saying they were his, and then I lost my temper. I took the crackers, ripped open the package, and stuffed them into his mouth, yelling, "You wanted these crackers. Now you are going to eat them."

I'm not proud of it, but considering the stress I was under, I lost it. The next morning, I was at work, and the school called and said I had to come to the school immediately. I explained that I was working as a waitress and since it was almost lunchtime, I would not be able to come right now, and the counselor at the school said if I did not come right now, they would call DYFS because Marcy told the counselor her stepmother choked her brother and she was afraid to go home. I couldn't believe it. Now I left work immediately, causing my boss to be very angry with me and also not being able to make the much-needed money from the lunch rush. I went first to Marcy's school and told what happened, then I had to go to Jackie's school and give my side of the story to his school counselor. Thankfully, both counselors understood and did not feel it was abuse. I only made him eat the crackers. The way Marcy told the story, they thought I figuratively choked him. Still, Pete did not take my side, even though I screamed at him that if they thought the kids were abused, they could take Nadine away.

That was not my only visit with a school counselor with accusation of child abuse. In 1987 Sammy was a junior in North Bergen High School, and I received a call from her school counselor saying they needed to see me and her father immediately. Pete just happened to be away at a training session for his job, so I left my job and went up to the high school not knowing what it was about. I got there and was greeted by a counselor who did not even introduce herself. She just told me to sit down and that she was giving me the courtesy of explaining what was going on in our home. She told me that Sammy had advised her that the reason her grades were so bad was that she was tired because she worked during the night and then came to work with little sleep and that she also took care of her little brother and sister when she wasn't working. She had mentioned that I was a drinker and very often was drunk, so she had to make dinner on top of everything else and that her dad was always upset because he couldn't find a job.

The counselor also invited the vice principal into the meeting because whenever there was an accusation of abuse, they needed to have it documented. I was completely shocked and had no idea where all this was coming from. I told her that none of this was true. I was not a drinker, although I did enjoy a drink with dinner when we would go out. I also told her that I was a legal secretary at Jersey City Law Department and her father was not unemployed; as a matter of fact, the reason he could not be at the meeting was because he was at a training session in Virginia to learn a new phone system for his job. And as for her having to take care of a younger brother and sister, that also was untrue. Both children lived with their mom, and we only saw them every other weekend. I could tell that the counselor was not sure whom to believe, then I had mentioned that my daughter was a freshman at North Bergen and was an honor roll student. The vice principal asked me to wait in another room while they called Claudette down.

She did not know I was in the other room and, of course, told them exactly what I had said. Sammy did not work in the evenings. There was no alcoholism, and no, the children did not live with us. After sending her back to class, they called Sammy down and asked me back into the room. When she saw me there, her face dropped. Then the counselor and the vice principal recommended that we go to counseling as a family, which we did for the next couple of months. It was at that time they found out she had also told a lot of other untrue stories. Claudette very often had to correct stories that other students would ask her about. After attending counseling with Sammy and hearing a lot of what she said we figured that she lacked a feeling of importance, maybe because her mom gave her up and maybe that was the reason she made up the stories.

When you live a life of yours, mine, and ours, it is quite an interesting life. Claudette absolutely despised Pete and often would purposely cross him with regard to his rules, especially staying in the bathroom too long in the mornings, causing him to always run late, always talking back to him, saying, "You're not my father. I don't have to listen to you. Pete tried to be extra nice to her in the beginning knowing how she felt, but when pressured, even she could not say why she did not like him.

When I met Pete, I fell hook, line, and sinker. Even when well-meaning friends would try to point out difficulties that might occur with a blended family, I wouldn't listen. He had been married twice, had children from both marriage, and got custody of the kids both times. To me this just made me fall even deeper in love. Any man that would get custody in court twice must be a great guy was the way I looked at it. Not realizing that meant that I would be getting custody of these kids if the relationship moved forward.

When Marcy and Jackie were twelve and ten, respectively, we received a call from his Brooke's husband stating that she left him and left the kids with him. I guess he realized that legally, he was not able to keep the kids, so he turned them over to us.

Back to court again, only this time, it was us bringing the case. We received custody, and she didn't come around for ten months. After her divorce from husband number two, she remarried and showed up, wanting the kids back. Now the kids were old enough to choose, and they begged to go back with her. Only problem was, her new husband and she moved out of state, almost eight hours away.

This meant that our visitation with Marcy and Jackie was quite limited to summer. Brooke and Pete agreed that he didn't have to pay weekly support, instead just pay for their back-to-school clothing and any sports-related fees. Although he was not happy about not seeing them every other weekend, he did agree. I, on the other hand was not as upset. Finally, we were going to be just him, me, and Nadine.

Sammy was married, and Claudette got an apartment in Rutherford. I was finally going to live the life I used to only dream about. Me, my husband, and our daughter—I thought it was going to be great, but it was short-lived. The house we rented had gotten sold, so we had to move, then after living in a new house with our six-year-old for only a couple of months, we had a fire in the house, and we had to move into the hotel where I worked as a night auditor for ninety-nine days. Lucky for us, we got to stay there free of charge. We then found a nice small cottage to rent. I was thoroughly enjoying the time with just the three of us, then a phone call on Father's Day: "Hey, Dad, happy Father's Day," Jackie said. "I was wondering if I could come and live with you and Bernice permanently."

Needless to say, we now got full custody of Jackie, who was no longer the sweet ten-year-old that moved back with his mom in December 1995. Instead, he came back an angry, mean-spirited fourteen-year-old boy who was not used to rules and regulations. His mom never even objected to his decision. He was totally disrespectful to me and treated Nadine horribly. He chose to ignore her at all cost. Here we had this little girl who was so excited to have her brother back, and he didn't want anything to do with her. My heart went out to Nadine because her childhood was so confusing to her. There were times she was one of five kids, then the kids went home, and Sammy and Claudette no longer lived home, so she was an only child, then in the summer months, back to being one of three and back to being only child, then when Jackie came home, back to being one of two. It's no wonder that she had gone through depression when she was a teenager. As much as I tried and most of the times thought I was doing a good job being a good mother to her and a fairly and good stepmother to Jackie, I'm sure I fell short. Superwoman I am not.

In my effort to be a decent stepmother, my own daughter was suffering right under my nose, and I missed it.

Once again I was failing my daughter by not giving her the attention she deserved. Today I am sometimes saddened by the comments Nadine makes, like how I was never there for her. I'm not exactly sure of what more I could have done. Everything I did as a mother, it was done out of my love and the feelings of my need to care for her.

Claudette also makes comments about how bad she had it as a child. It really blows my mind how differently people see the same situation. From my perspective, I gave her a great life with what I had. I got her away from an abusive situation, leaving her dad at 12:30 a.m. with no shoes on and a ripped dress; we escaped the home after he beat me about the head with a ketchup bottle. We walked three blocks to my brother's house. When I left my abusive marriage, I was twenty-two years old with a three-year-old, scared out of my mind. My first job was hiding from Dave, who was abusive and did not give up easily. After the divorce papers were filed, I went back to my job full-time and moved in with my two brothers while I saved for an apartment for me and Claudette; also, it was safer. Dave tried everything to try to get me to change my mind, even going so far as to pick Claudette up from nursery school without my permission and kept her hidden at a friend's house overnight. Then he tried getting his mom to testify in court, saying he could not afford too much child support because he was helping out at home. He told the judge I didn't need the money because I was living with two guys, not mentioning that the two guys were my own brothers. Claudette was so upset about him not being around, and she would very often cry and say, "If you did not burn the steak and french fries and string beans, Daddy would not have gotten mad, and we would still live with him."

As young as she was, it would often amaze me of the things she remembered. Another time, he complained about the stain in the rug, so I shampooed it and the next day yelled at Claudette for bringing a glass of milk into the parlor so she would not spill her milk on the clean rug. He got so mad that I yelled at her. He took a gallon of milk and poured it in the middle of it. In addition to the physical abuse, he was often very good at emotional abuse too, telling me constantly about his friend's wife being a better cook or making more money than me, how he was embarrassed being married to me. Claudette very often would repeat some of the things she would hear, saying, "If you cooked better, Daddy would live with us," or, "If you were pretty, Daddy would live here." I guess it was easier than to believe he really didn't want to be with her.

I tried so hard to be a good mother, but I must admit I was a little too hard on her. Being such a young mother, I was always worried that people would think I was not a good mother, so as I look back now, I realize I was too hard on her.

Oh, My Daughter Is Going to College

On August 26, 1991, my nerves were completely shot. I just could not calm down. *Claudette is leaving for college tomorrow. How can that be? I have had this enormous lump in my throat all day. Is it from happiest with pride or saddest that she is going away to college? It's not like she is going across the country. She will be in Montclair, and we live at least for the new couple of days in North Bergen, about twenty-five minutes away. Then the next day I will be moving along with my husband and two-year-old daughter and nineteen-year-old stepdaughter, Sammy, up to Vernon, still only about forty minutes away, but it still feels too far away.* The day started with me trying to think of other things so as not to cry in front of her; she was so happy and excited she could barely contain herself when we received a call from her best friend's mom asking if I could drive her daughter to the college as her mother-in-law was dying and she and her husband had to get to the hospital.

I packed my '61 Chevy with all of Claudette's belongings then headed over to Michele's to pack her things as well; we filled the car with two TVs, two microwaves, two sets of beddings, as well as hair supplies and tons of clothes, and two very excited college students. I guess the distraction was working because I had not shed a tear and thought I might actually be able to get through it all before I lost it. The girls were excitedly talking about classes and campus life and how much fun they were going to have as I was driving along Route 3 in Clifton, just about five minutes away from the college, when suddenly there was a thud, and the car quickly stopped dead in its tracks. The front wheel of the passenger side of the car came off the car, causing me to swerve to the left, at three thirty on a Thursday workday, just starting rush hour. I was almost blocking both lanes of the highway. Of course, this was long before cell phones. Both girls were freaking out about being late and fearing that they would not be able to move into their dorms on time. I quickly told them to get out of the car and get behind the guardrail for safety, then I walked up the road and climbed up a small hill to the Ford dealership so I could use their phone. I called a tow truck and then called my sister Bernadette, hoping she would be able to come and take the girls to the college while I dealt with the car.

Then I called the college to explain the delay, and they said there was only a certain time they could check in and if we didn't get there in time, we would have to come back after Labor Day. This was exactly what I needed to add to the stress. I walked back to the car and watched from the side of the road while some of the traffic squeezed around my car. Trying to calm the girls, I was telling them Aunt Bernadette was on her way, but under my breath, I was praying she would get there in time to allow them enough time to check into their dorms.

Finally, the tow truck got there, and Bernadette was just two cars behind it. We had a nice driver who helped us pack the girls' things into Bernadette's van and understood the dilemma. I rode with Bernadette, got the girls to the college with only ten minutes to spare before the move-in time had ended. Bernadette promised to come back to pick me up after getting her kids from their sitter.

Michelle's dorm was on one side of the campus, while Claudette's was on the other. Thank God I was still young at that time, because I helped Claudette get settled then ran to Michelle's to make sure she was set up. After both girls were settled into their dorms and excited to start their college careers, I waited for Bernadette to pick me up, void of any emotions, just totally exhausted and concerned about the car. *How much is this going to cost? Is it going to be fixed by the time I got there?*

What a great guy. When I walked into the repair shop, I was met with a big smile, saying the car was ready; he changed the tire, as well as put on a new rim. Then he handed me the bill. As I glanced down, I was in shock.

He said, "No charge, good luck to the college girls."

That evening after getting Nadine settled in bed and Pete was off to his bowling night, I finally crashed. As I pulled the covers down, I found a card from Claudette. In the card, she thanked me for giving her life and raising her and bringing her to this most exciting day of her life thus far. She went on to give me examples of when I was there for her and how much she loved me. That's when I lost it. I must have cried for hours—tears of pride, tears of sadness, tears of frustration. I wonder if the car situation had happened to spare her the embarrassment of having me lose it at the college. Funny how things happen. I am now and always have been so very proud of her. She turned into an amazing adult and is now a social worker.

It seems like college trips are not exactly my thing. Fast-forward fifteen years, and another college trip nightmare.

June 2007, Nadine was about to go off to East Carolina University Greenville North Carolina. *Wow, where has the time gone?* She got accepted to her first-choice school, and I could not have been happier. It was orientation weekend, and Pete, myself, and Nadine packed the van and set out for the three-day trip to North Carolina. Nadine was to have two-day orientation, where she was going to stay overnight at the college and meet her college roommate, and Pete and I had a reservation at the local Days Inn. The excitement was contagious. She was up and showered and ready to go by the time I opened my eyes. The three of us got into the car, stopped for a breakfast, which she begged we eat in the car so we did not waste too much time. It was going to be a ten-hour trip, so we agreed.

We stopped only for lunch and a couple of gas and bathroom breaks and were enjoying our time with one another, and then the nightmare started.

In Virginia, we heard a noise coming from the van, and then it shut down. Luckily, we were close to an exit and cruised off the exit right into a Days Inn parking lot. The van would not turn back on, so we checked into the hotel. Of course, Nadine was hysterical.

"How are we going to make it to my school?" she cried over and over.

I kept reminding her that we should be happy no one got hurt and we would figure it out. But as anyone who has an eighteen-year-old knows, the world resolves only around them, and no one or nothing else is of importance. It was dark by this time, so the only thing to do was get a little sleep and deal with it in the morning. I spent the night looking up car repair places in the phone book and trying unsuccessfully to get some sleep. At 7:00 a.m., I finally got hold of an AAMCO station and spoke with a repairman who said it sounded like the transmission had seized and he would be able to fix it but it would take two days. They agreed to send a tow truck to pick up the van, but it would be a couple hours before they would be able to get there as they were so busy. When the driver arrived, he told us to sit in the car and then he put the car up on the truck, and we drove for forty-five minutes that way. It was quite scary, but what else could we do? When we got to the AAMCO dealership, the estimate was $1,300, and they promised to have it done in two days. There was a rental car place adjacent to their shop, so we rented a car and got back on the road. I called the Days Inn we had reservations in Greenville, North Carolina, and explained what happened and said we would not be able to check in on time but that we would definitely need the room when we got there. We originally reserved the room for two nights. I agreed that even though we did not stay the two rights, I would definitely pay for two. He said fine. Unfortunately, I did not get his name.

Now with everything packed into the rental car, we were once again on the road, but we were definitely no longer in such a festive mood. We drove through the night and arrived at the Days Inn in Greenville just about 6:30 a.m. When we tried to check in, we were told they no longer had our room because we did not check in when we were scheduled to. Of course, I explained that I had called, but they said they had no record of my call. I left there and tried checking into another hotel, only to be told that every place was booked because of the orientation at the college. Needless to say, this situation did not sit too well with Nadine. She started to cry and carry on how she could not be late for orientation and since we were driving all night and she needed to shower and change her clothes. We continued to go in and out of every hotel explaining our situation. One woman whose name was Tracey was very sympathetic and allowed Nadine to use the employees' rest room to clean up and change her clothes and also asked for my cell phone number and told me she would call me if they had a cancellation.

Then we went to the college for the orientation, which started five minutes after we arrived, leaving no time for breakfast. The lecture hall was completely full of anxious college students and their parents. It was hard trying to find three seats together for us. Finally, we saw three seats in the middle of the of an aisle. We needed to excuse ourselves, passed a lot of people to get to the middle. I was desperately trying to calm down and focus on the information the dean of schools was giving in his speech when suddenly my cell phone vibrated. When I looked at it, I noticed it was from the AAMCO dealer, so I excused myself, passed all the people sitting there, and then called him back; he told me the transmission was going to cost $3,500 to fix, not $1,300 because when they took it out, it was more than he expected. I figured he was trying to take advantage, so I called my mechanic in New Jersey to ask for his advice, and he said, "No, do not pay it. Have the van towed home and I can fix it for a lot less."

I called the AAMCO dealer and told him we did not want to let him fix it.

I got the evil eye from Nadine as well as everyone else I had to pass on my way back to my seat and tried to quietly explain to Pete what was happening with the van when my cell phone vibrated again. This time it was the lady from the Quality Inn. Good news she has a room for us, but she needed my credit card number to hold the room. I had to give her my credit card number, so I once again had to excuse myself out of the seat. This time I was not going to go back to my seat and listened to the rest of the dean's speech from the back of hall. After a while, it was time for the parents and the students to separate and then meet again at lunchtime. Nadine would not even look at me and said I embarrassed her by getting in and out of my seat while the dean was talking; there was no use trying to defend my decisions. As hard as I tried, I could not concentrate on anything that was being said about Nadine's college life; it made me feel like a horrible mother. I tried asking Nadine all about her meetings and her schedule and tried to act really excited, trying not to think about the mess we were in, only talking about the school, but she would not budge. She was furious with me. Somehow Pete escaped the fury because I was the one who was trying to fix everything. After lunch, the parents' meetings were over, and the students had to go to meet with their roommates for their first night to sleep at the dorms.

I explained everything to Pete about our mechanic saying we should tow the van home and we had to find the U-Haul to rent to haul the car home. We went to the computer lab to ask to use the computers. We were told they were only to be used for checking on financial aid. So of course, that's what I told them, that I had to check Nadine's financial aid. It took about an hour, but I finally reserved a truck and tow to get our van back to New Jersey. So Nadine was at the school waiting to meet her roommate, and the U-Haul was reserved, and all the meetings were over, so Pete and I drove back to the hotel with the hopes for a nice dinner and a much-needed drink.

Just as we were pulling into the hotel parking lot, the phone rang. It was the U-Haul company. Apparently, they had a truck and a tow available, but unfortunately, they were in two separate locations; one was in Lexington, and one in Alexandria, not knowing anything about Virginia or the proximity of the two locations I said okay. Then as I hung up, Nadine called in tears. Her roommate did not show up, and she did not want to sleep at the college by herself, and she asked if we could pick her up. So much for a nice dinner and drink. We drove back to the college, and as we pulled in, Nadine called back; her roommate just got there, and she was really nice, so she said she wanted to stay.

"Well, we are here now," I told Pete. "We might as well look up on the computers for the directions to pick up the truck and tow."

It turned out they were quite a distance from one another and would probably add an additional five hours on to our trip home. Just as we were leaving the campus, I saw a sign for a comedian, and all was welcome. "Well, we can certainly use a laugh. Let's stay and see it I feel like I'm going to blow, and maybe we could get a glimpse of Nadine and see if she is having a good time."

Luckily, we saw her, but she did not see us, and she looked like she was happy and having a good time, so I felt better about leaving her at the dorm.

Totally exhausted, we stopped at the gas station and picked up sandwiches on the way back to the hotel, and guess what was right across the street from our hotel. A U-Haul dealer. Although they were closed, we could clearly see a truck and a tow right there in the lot. Oh my god, I couldn't believe it, just what we needed. The only problem was that they opened at 8:00 a.m., and that was the same time as the parent-and-student breakfast. We anguished over it all night but decided it was more important to miss the breakfast and get the truck and tow. Needless to say, Nadine did not agree with us. We reserved the truck and tow and paid for it and got to the cafeteria just as they were announcing for everyone to meet in the lecture hall for the dean's goodbye and good-luck speech. She was so mad at us, saying she was the only one without her parents there and she was so embarrassed. As much as I know this was a big time in her life and she really was upset, I finally cracked. I told her I had enough of her attitude; none of this was our fault, and we all had to make the best of a tough situation. I guess I got to her because she backed down and we went to the lecture hall arm and arm. This was a speech I was able to pay attention to and started to feel the excitement of Nadine going to college.

The parents were supposed to wait at the cafeteria as the students got their IDs and got to go over their schedules. Pete and I were eating lunch when I looked at the receipt for the U-Haul and saw it was going to close at four; it was already three ten, and no sign of Nadine. I started to ask everyone in sight if they knew where the incoming freshman were having their IDs taken, then I saw the dean who had spoken early in the day. I stopped him and started to stress out about not being about to find my daughter, and he smiled and said he knew I was a nervous parent but just wait at the cafeteria; that was where the students were instructed to meet their parents. I explained our situation through tears, and he said go to the U-Haul, pick up the truck, and he would track Nadine down and wait with her at the cafeteria until we got back.

I called the U-Haul place and told them we were on our way, but he said, "We are closing in five minutes, so just pick it up in the morning."

I started to cry so hard the guy could barely understand what I was saying, but he had a heart and did say he would wait for me. We got there, and the U-Haul was closed, but the guy was waiting for us in the driveway with the keys and assisted us in putting the rental car on the tow. I was so appreciative I gave him a big hug and a tip. As he got in his car and waved to us, Pete got into the driver's side, and I got into the passenger side, and that was when we noticed it was not a bench seat for three people but two console bucket seat with a space in between. OH MY GOD. *There is no place for Nadine to sit.*

I started to cry unconsolably, and Pete said, "Don't worry. We will figure something out," and pulled out of the driveway.

You could just imagine Nadine's face when she was standing there with the dean of the college and we pulled onto campus with a tow truck with car in tow. We got out of the truck and thanked him for staying with her, waited for him to walk away before we told Nadine that she needed to put her pillows in the middle of the two seats and sit there for the ride home. I think she knew we had been through enough stress, so she just climbed in and talked excitedly about the school and her classes and kept her discomfort to herself.

By the time we arrived at the AAMCO in Virginia, it was 12:30 a.m., and as we arranged with the owner of the shop that he would leave the keys in the floor of the van so Pete and I got the rental car off the tow, and we put the keys of the rental in the slot, but moving the van with the transmission on the back seat was a little bit harder. Pete and I were pushing the van as Nadine was trying to steer the van onto the tow when suddenly bright lights glared at us and the police started telling us not to move and asked what we were doing.

They called the owner up, and we had to wait for him to come vouch for us and said that we agreed that we would be picking up the van. He then assisted us getting the van onto the tow using an electric jack. Because Nadine was such a good sport sitting on pillows for hours I volunteered to let her sit in the seat for the rest of the ride home, but she said no and got herself comfortable enough to actually fall asleep for a couple of hours.

Fifteen hours after leaving ECU, we pulled into our driveway. Nadine went right to bed, and unfortunately, Pete had to go to work. I called my sister Bernadette, who once again came to my aid.

"What are you doing?" I said. "How about take me car shopping?"

I went from car dealer to car dealer until I found a car I could afford and get approved for a brand-new car that no one else had ever owned, a car that would not break down and one that did not have a transmission on its back seat.

For the first time in my life, I bought a brand-new car, a Chevy HHR. When I drove it home, Pete had been home from work already and was asleep. I knew he would be upset, but after everything I had been through in the last three days, I could take it. The reason I bought HHR was because it looked like an old car, so as much as he would be mad, he might be less mad if it was an old-looking style.

Two months later when Nadine moved into her dorm as a freshman, we drove down in style without the worry of breaking down.

Looking back on these trips, I certainly can laugh, but going through them was quite another story.

Love You to Death

When I was a little girl, I had a dream, which was probably the same dream as many other girls. My dream was to marry a wonderful man and have children and a car and a house and live happily ever after.

At the age of eighteen, my dream was about to come true. I found out I was pregnant and my high school sweetheart, Dave, took that dream and turned it into a nightmare. At first, he was very happy about the baby and said, "Let's get married," and I was so very excited.

My mom was so mad about my situation that she could not even talk to me for approximately two weeks, then on my nineteenth birthday, she decided to have lunch with me and finally told me that she had hoped I had more sense than to get pregnant, and she also told me she did not expect Dave to be a good husband or father. She felt I sealed the deal for a hard life in the future. After lunch, she and I went to an appliance store, and she purchased a big refrigerator that was far more expensive than I would have chosen, and she said that she wanted me to have at least something nice because she did not expect Dave would be able to give me nice things.

On January 13, 1973, with the help of family members, wedding invitations and thank-you cards were a gift from Dave's brother, Charlie, and his wife, Barbara; the band was paid for by my sister Carolyn; a gift of liquor and soda was supplied by my brother Edward, who also walked me down the aisle of Saint Paul's of the Cross church. Decorations were provided by my sister Margaret, all of which made for a beautiful wedding reception held at the Shannon Bar in Hoboken, also a gift from the owner who was my mom's friend.

We rented an extremely nice apartment. Security was paid as a wedding gift by two of my brothers, Raymond and Richard, and I was unrealistically confident my marriage was going to be wonderful, just like I always dreamed.

The statement "Mother knows best" was never a truer statement than in regard to my marriage; it was bad almost from day one. The day after we got married, it just happened to be Super Bowl Sunday. How could Dave miss such an important game? So I spent the day after my wedding playing waitress to a bunch of guys in my apartment who came by to watch Super Bowl. Most of our friends were not married and did not have their own place, so my apartment soon became a hangout place for his friends to watch football games almost every Sunday, and since he worked the midnight shift at the post office, he could not very well go to work after drinking all day. Unfortunately, in 1973, the drinking age was only eighteen, which was part of the reason for Dave missing so much work, causing him many times to be suspended without pay from his job.

When football season was over, so were my hopes of a little bit of quality time with my husband, because baseball season started up with him joining a team with the neighborhood bar. If they won, he couldn't go to work because he would celebrate after the game and could not very well go to work. If they lost, he would also drown his sorrow and miss work. There were times that his friend's girlfriend would call him out of work pretending to be me. I would be surprised when he would come in around 2:00 a.m. saying work was slow so they sent him home. Most of the times I would not know how much work he missed until he bought his paycheck home.

When I was seven months pregnant, the physical abuse started with no warning of what would set him off. It could be something like, he wanted something to eat, or the house was not cleaned to his liking. Sometimes, he would invite friends over, without any knowledge of whether or not we had food in the refrigerator.

On some occasions, he would come home so angry about something that I had nothing to do with, but taking his anger out on me with his fist was the way he dealt with it. This time the landlord did call the cops. When the cops arrived, Dave was able to talk his way out of trouble by recognizing one of the cops as one of the teammates from a baseball game he was involved with. It was suggested that I go for a walk till he calmed down. The fact that it was 10:00 p.m. on a Saturday night and I was pregnant did not matter.

This was the beginning of the physical abuse, usually followed by flowers and apologies and even some claims of not remembering anything he did.

I would try to be counteractive, always making sure there was food in the house easy enough to cook quickly in case he came home hungry and always tried to make sure the house was spotless, even though I was always exhausted, working a full-time job and taking care of a baby and also doing some typing at home for an ambulance company's billings to make extra money.

One day he overslept and instead of having him rush and be late for work, I just called his job and said he was sick. I knew he had been out with friends that afternoon and had too much to drink, so I figured he would be okay with it. But boy was I wrong. He got up and started screaming and yelling, throwing things all over, saying he could not afford to have any time from work and that if he got suspended, it would be my fault. Apparently, he had been taking off a lot more than he let on, so he called the job and told his boss he was feeling better so he would be in.

I didn't sleep a wink, worried how he was going to be when he got home. With absolutely no sleep, I got Claudette to the nursey school then went to work barely able to think of anything other than what was going to happen when I got home. To my surprise, he was so nice telling me over and over how he knew I meant well. I never knew what to expect.

Some abuse has bruises that don't quite heal. The constant belittlement of being told over and over "You're ugly," "You're skinny," "You're a bad cook," "No one likes you," and "You are lucky to have me" can wear a person down. It wasn't long before I started to believe everything he said.

When we were invited to his friend's wedding, I purchased a dress and spent a lot of time getting ready. I wanted to make sure I looked good for him. I curled my hair with a hot iron and thought my hair looked so nice. I wanted him to be proud of me. We were having a good time, dancing and eating and talking to the other guest at the table, then one of his friends commented that my hair looked pretty.

Suddenly Dave said, "Let's go. I want to go home."

We had such a great time I was thinking he just wanted to be alone with me. I was looking forward to going home also. I was in total shock that once he got home, he went immediately to the bedroom, got the curling iron, and started breaking it into many pieces while screaming that I was flirting with everyone.

Shortly after that incident, we received another invitation to one of his friend's wedding, and worrying about not having a repeat of the last, I decided I would not go to the wedding with him. So, at the last minute, I told him the babysitter cancelled, but he should go anyway. I was pretty confident all would be well when he came home, but I was wrong. Apparently, he had a rotten time; everyone was with their wives, and he was mad that I was not there, and he left before dinner and was now hungry. So once again, I had to scramble up something to eat that was to his liking, which was not happening, which gave him an excuse to start hitting and insulting me over and over.

There were so many incidences where I had to lie about my bruises, such as being hit with a baseball at the park, or I got stitches in my head because I had hit the top drawer while putting away clothes.

It's such a common response when someone hears about a woman being a battered wife; the first thing they say is, "Why does she stay?" not "Why does he beat her?" It is a feeling that somehow it is your fault. As hard as I tried, I could never figure out how to act. If I cried when he hit, me he would say I was weak. If I fought back, he only hit harder. There were times he would apologize, and other times, he would claim he did not remember anything. Other times he would say I deserved it.

I thought about leaving many times, but I really had nowhere to go and thought he would eventually change, but I was wrong.

It took me four years to get up the courage to leave this situation once it appeared the violence was not going to stop and that this kind of life would affect Claudette as she grew up. This was the hardest and most rewarding thing I have ever done in my life, and years later, I was part of the CRT Response team working to help other battered wives.

Although there is absolutely nothing funny about domestic violence, there was one incident that occurred that was a little humorous. I saw an article in our local advertiser that Sussex County College was having a two-day workshop on domestic violence and was looking for volunteers to run it. After hearing that I was a survivor of domestic violence myself, the coordinator asked if I would give a speech.

Unbeknownst to me, there was a reporter there from our local TV station, and I was asked for permission to have my speech aired on TV, which was aired several times during the week. On Friday evening, my husband Pete and I went to our son's football dinner. While there, Pete had mentioned to me that many people were giving him the cold shoulder. We have been friends with these people all football season. As a matter of fact, we even have been out to dinner with a couple of the other parents. We were surprised also of the fact that even though there was no assigned seating, no one was coming to sit at our table. The coach came over to say hello and mentioned he had seen me on TV, and that was when we realized it.

The workshop was a two-part series. My first part of the speech, which was about being a battered wife and how hard it was to get out of the situation and how hard it was because to the outside world, my husband was such a good guy, the life of the party, but behind closed doors, he was quite abusive; in my speech, which aired that week, I said that the most dangerous time for a battered wife is when they try to leave, and most women just stayed in the marriage.

The second part of the speech, which had not aired yet, was how I managed to get out and how there is definitely life after domestic violence and how I was now married to a wonderful man who wouldn't hurt a fly.

The coach asked why we were not sitting with anyone, and I mentioned maybe they saw the speech and thought Pete was an abusive husband. That was when he said, "Don't worry." He grabbed a pizza box and made a big sign that said, "I'M NOT THE ONE. I'M HUSBAND NUMBER 2."

And he put it on our table for all to see. Gradually, the other parents came over.

"THERE IS LIFE AFTER DOMESTIC VIOLENCE."

I hope each and every person who is in a relationship will know that LOVE IS NOT SUPPOSED TO HURT.

Lost in the Crowd

So often I hear many people talk about their parents and some great memories of their childhood or reflect on words of wisdom they got from their parents, and it makes me think back to my own childhood. Do I also have these same memories?

Do I often rely on some great advice that was given to me from my parents?

What lessons did I learn from them that shaped me into who I am today?

As sad as it seems, the harder I try, I can only think of a handful of occasions when I had any one-on-one conversations with either of my parents. There are ten of us children in the family, and I am also a twin, so individual attention was very rare, except when it was report card day. I was a very bad student. My report cards were like American flag red, white and blue, red for P (poor), which was most academic grades, blue for attendance and gym, which was on a white background. On report card night, I got a lot of attention, not the kind I craved, mostly screaming about why I got such bad marks when my twin did so much better, why didn't I let her help me if I didn't understand; after all, we were in the same grade. They just didn't understand how hard it was to always have to live in Bernadette's shadow; it seemed everything she touched turned into gold even at a very young age. She learned how to sew and knit and crochet, and of course, she also did very well in school. The only thing I had going for me was that I was that I was very athletic and excelled in gym class, which did not impress my mom.

When Bernadette and I were graduating eighth grade, I was told I was getting an award recognizing my high scores in gym. I was supposed to get recognized on Exit Day. I waited breathlessly and watched the audience for my mother so excited that finally I had something my mother would be proud of me for, but she did not come. I received my award, which suddenly didn't seem so important as I scanned the audience for my missing mom. When I got home, I asked why she didn't come.

Her reply was, "Oh, it was just gym."

The next day was graduation day, and I was so excited that I had squeaked through enough to graduate, and then it was time for my name to be called, and the boy calling out names accidently said Bernadette Datz instead of Bernice Datz while I was standing there. I burst into tears and hurried off the stage. After we left the school, everyone, including my mom, laughed about the incorrect name and said I should calm down; as long as the correct name was on the diploma, it was fine.

Unfortunately for me, many of the memories I have of my mom are not the warm and fuzzy conversations I have heard others reminisce about.

On March 5, 1964, my mom did not wake us up for school, so when I got up and asked her why she did not wake us up and we were going to be late, she quietly told me to wake up everyone and tell us to come into the kitchen. When all eight of us were there, she told us that "Daddy went to heaven and we did not have to go to school that day."

I was ten years old at that time and remember my first thought was, "I'm ashamed to say, who was going to sign my papers when I failed?" My dad was so much kinder to me whenever I approached him to sign a failing test, always asking me to promise I would do better next time, whereas when my mom was the one to sign, it usually was accompanied with a lot of yelling and sometimes getting hit and comparing me to my twin sister, who never failed anything. After my dad's unexpected death of a cerebral hemorrhage, my mom had to raise us with little money, so she went to work as a nurse's aide in the hospital where she became friends with other women who were either widowed or divorced.

Gradually, she would stop with these other women at the local bar. At that time, women had to sit in the back room, not the actual bar, but that did not deter them from drinking, and eventually, she became an alcoholic. With so much pressure of raising us without any help, I can see now how hard it must have been on her. I'm sure we did not make it easy on her. There was a time when she had six teenagers in a small four-room apartment, a son in the Army, and two sons and a daughter who were married with families of their own, so I can just imagine how tough it was for her considering she was only forty-nine years old when she became a widow.

I remember when I was seventeen years old and our curfew was 10:00 p.m., I was home on time, but Bernadette was not, which was very unusual for her. My mom kept looking out the window and commenting how unusual it was that Bernadette would be late.

I said, "Oh, she is probably just hanging out and forgot the time."

By 10:35 p.m., she was beside herself and told me to go look for her.

I said, "Mom, what are you so worried about? Lots of times when I'm late, you don't send anyone out looking for me."

She got so angry and just yelled, "Just go look for her. Something might have happened to her."

I was so upset and left the house thinking she did not care about me; it would serve her right that something should happen to me just to show her. Well, it didn't take me long. Bernadette was just up the corner talking to her new boyfriend. When we got home, she was telling my mom how excited she was that Ray asked her out and was going on and on, no talk of punishment or anything. Mom was so happy that Bernadette had had a boyfriend since I had the same boyfriend since freshman year.

Throughout my teen years until I got married, I did not have much of a relationship with my mom. I guess I was so wrapped up in my own life I never considered her feelings. When her drinking got out of control, very often we would be called to go pick her up from the bar, and there were times when I was so embarrassed by her I now look back and feel so bad about it.

One day she came to the restaurant where she knew I usually had lunch with my coworkers. When she came in, her wig was crooked, and you can tell she was hung over. I was sitting at a table with a couple of coworkers, which included three salesmen and two secretaries. It was secretaries' day and also my mon's birthday, which is why she was in Hoboken. She was on her way to meet her friend and was early so decided to surprise me since it was lunchtime. I was so embarrassed I did not even introduce her when she approached the table. It reminds me of Diana Ross's song "Living in Shame." Now when I look back, I can't even remember the names of the people who were there, but I do remember the look on her face waiting to be introduced to my friends as I ushered her toward the door. How I wish I could go back to that day and say, "This is my mom." As a mom myself, I think she was a lot stronger than I could have ever been giving the circumstances. She raised ten children, all successful adults who have never been in any kind of trouble, one son who was in the Navy, and one who was in the Army serving in Vietnam. Four of us had our own businesses, seven of us own our own homes, and there are twenty-nine grandchildren, twenty-two great-grand-children, and nine great-great-grandchildren, and we are all close, so I'm sure she did something right.

She passed away at the tender age of fifty-nine, and I really miss her. I was quite distraught at the time of her passing. She was in the hospital for eight months, and I, as well as my siblings, were up the hospital quite often. As a matter fact, my daughter Claudette took her first steps in the hospital as my mom looked on from the bed. The nurses used to keep an eye on her in the hallway because they did not allow her in the room. The nurse held the door open while I let go of the baby's hand as she started to walk. Still remember how excited my mom was. That was August 1.

On August 21, 1974, I was on my way to the hospital, not sure which mom would be there. Would it be the mom who wanted to know about my day or the mom who didn't even know who I was and would be talking about things that made absolutely no sense? Cirrhosis of the liver is the kind of disease that often affects the brain. When I got to the hospital, I was pleasantly surprised to find that my mom was her old self. As a matter of fact, she was hungry and said she was in the mood for a ham sandwich with mustard. When I asked the nurse, she said, "Oh no, your mom is on a liquid diet. She cannot have the sandwich."

When I told her what the nurse said, she really was like my old mom, that's for sure. "I don't care what the nurse said. I am your mother, and I am telling you to get me a ham sandwich with mustard."

Well, I went down to the cafeteria and got the sandwich and hid it in my pocket so the nurse did not see it. I broke the sandwich in little pieces, and she ate almost half of it, saying how much she enjoyed it. I was so enjoying her company, but I needed to get home and pick up Claudette from the sitter and then home to make dinner for my husband. On the bus ride home, I was thinking maybe she was getting better, maybe the doctors were wrong. I just couldn't wait to tell my brothers and sisters how well she was today.

As I walked into the door, the phone was ringing. "Hello, Bernice. This is Dr. Howard. I'm sorry to tell you, but your mom is expiring, and you and your siblings should come to the hospital as soon as possible."

I quickly yelled to my husband to get his sister to babysit when it was time for him to go to work if I wasn't back in time. Waiting forever for a bus, I finally flagged down a police car and begged them to take me to the hospital, hoping they would drive quickly and put on the siren, but they didn't and even stopped to give someone a ticket for double parking. I could barely breathe. When I got into the room, I rushed to the bed, and my mom looked up at me with lifeless eyes. Apparently, she passed five minutes before I got there.

During the wake while endlessly greeting friends and family who came to pay their respects, it suddenly dawned on me, *Oh my god, did she die because she ate the sandwich? Oh, why did I give it to her when the nurse said no.* I looked over at my brothers and sisters and wondered if they would hate me when they found out what I did. For the next couple of days, I could not eat or sleep. I was tortured by my thoughts of the sandwich and whether that was the cause of her death. Two days after the funeral, after another sleepless night, I went to the Rectory of Saint Paul of the Cross at 11:00 p.m. I rang the doorbell, and a priest I never met came to the door seeing me hysterical. "Come in," he said. "What is wrong? What brings you here at this time of the night?"

"Father," I said through sobs, "I think I killed my mother."

"Sit, my dear," he said. "How do you think you killed your mom?"

"With a ham sandwich and mustard," I cried.

This was one time I'm sure that the priest was glad they are sworn to not repeat what is said to them.

"Woman kills mom! Weapon: HAM SANDWICH WITH MUSTARD."

He made us each a cup of tea and asked me to explain what happened. I told him about visiting the hospital and how the nurse said she could not have the sandwich and I gave it to her anyway and she died the same night, just about an hour later.

"What is your name?"

"Bernice," I sobbed.

"Well, Bernice," he said, "just like there are two sides of a coin and two sides of a story, there are two ways of looking at this. You can think yes, the sandwich caused her demise, *or* you can think how lucky you were to have given her LAST WISH. It's all a matter of perspective."

Wow, the agony and torture I had put myself through these past few days had lifted, and suddenly, I felt like the luckiest person in the world. How many people get this opportunity? Thank you, Fr. Mathews, for bringing so much brightness into this dark night.

With regard to my father, he worked long hours as a truck driver, and when he was at home, we all clamored to get his attention. My memories of one-on-one are only twice. When I was seven years old, my report card was not very good. My mom was screaming constantly, berating me over and over about my grades, and finally, my dad picked me up and took me to my aunt's house to spend the night, which was very unusual for a school night. He talked to me gently in the car and made me promise him that I would study my words better and if I needed help, I would ask for it as many times as I needed until I understood.

One other time when I was ten years old, I was home from school with a cold. My dad bundled me up and made me promise to keep a secret. He said he was buying my mom a ring for their anniversary and needed to go to pick it up, but the car wouldn't start, so we needed to walk to the jewelry store, which was about half hour away. We walked hand in hand, and he showed me the ring, and I helped him hide it when we got home. Little did I know that in less than one month, he would pass away.

On the night of my mom's passing, I was the first one there, and the nurse removed the ring from her finger, saying it was much too pretty to bury with her. Now the secret that I'm still keeping is that I kept the ring, and still have without the knowledge of my brothers and sisters. I feel like I was lucky enough to be there when the ring was bought, and now looking at this ring brings back such great memories of a little ten-year-old girl enjoying walking with her dad hand in hand.

As a parent now myself, I worry about how I will be remembered by my children and stepchildren. Hope there are far too many memories to remember them all. Writing this now makes me want to run out and take each one of them individually and just make memories.

Claudette and I are close to an extent. We talk about things, although we are not alike in many ways. Politically speaking, we are definitely on opposite sides. Her childhood was in my opinion pretty good, but she often mentions how bad it was and how her memory is not good because she blanks out the bad stuff. I sometimes think we lived a different life. I left her abusive father when she was three. We first moved in with my two brothers, who treated her like a princess. She could do no wrong in her uncles' eyes.

She is not at all interested in becoming a mom, which really makes me wonder if it was because of me that she would decide to be childless. Did she think she would not be a good mom? I so loved being a mom, and as most moms we want the circle of life, first being a child then having a child and then watching your child have a child. I have three grandchildren from my stepchildren, and I do love them so, but I so badly want to look into the eyes of a baby and see my eyes looking back at me.

My desire to have a good relationship with my daughters is causing me so many sleepless nights. I have gone to counseling and discussed ways of making things better, but it was told to me that "if I did not own the problem, I could not fix it." My desire to have a good relationship will only happen if my children let me in. Nadine appears to be harboring some animosity toward me. She once told me that I wanted to be her best friend and it was never going to happen so unless she wants to help me understand what is bothering her, I cannot help our relationship.

So my dream will have to be that Claudette and Nadine and my stepchildren will one day realize how much I love them and hope that someday we will be closer. I also wonder if I need to reflect back on my relationship with my own mother and wonder if she felt the same way about our relationship.

It's amazing how motherhood can be both the most amazing feeling in the world and also can be the most painful.

Perseverance Is the Key

From the moment I saw that little machine in my shorthand class as a senior in high school, I was so mesmerized by the stenographic machine and excited about being a court reporter. It was all I talked about when I got home from school, but the excitement was short-lived when my mom said there was no money for school. With six brothers and sisters living in the home, the only thing I was expected to do after graduation was to get a job.

Ten years after graduating and experiencing a marriage, birth of my daughter, and then divorce and working as an office worker, the desire of becoming a court reporter was still fresh in my mind. But being a single mom, money to go to school certainly was not available once again.

While at a family party, I was trying to convince one of my nieces into going to court reporting school after graduating, but she was not interested. My brother John overheard the conversation and told me if I was still interested in going to court reporting school, he would help me out financially. He did not have to ask me twice. I jumped at the opportunity. Of course I could not go full-time because I was supporting my daughter, who at the time was eight years old without any help from her dad. I found a school that had evening classes on Monday and Thursday from six to nine.

Finally, I started to realize my dream of becoming a court reporter. On the first day of classes, there were thirty-seven students; the excitement was more than I could handle. No way did I realize how hard it was going to be. For the next year and seven months, I studied like crazy to keep up after working full-time job and raising my daughter, but I was confident it would all be worth it. But luck was not on my side because of the fact it was such a hard course, many students dropped out, and the school eventually dropped their evening classes because of low enrollment. Unable to transfer to the day program, I had to put my dream on hold.

It took a while to find another school offering these same classes in the evening, but finally, I was back at it, but once again, it was short-lived—that school also discontinued evening classes because of low enrollment only seven months after I started. That was in 1985.

Three years later, I was remarried, and my husband and I won a little money off the lottery, and I used the money to go back to school. I found a school that offered classes in the evenings, but this time, it was in New York City, so I definitely did not think the school would close because of low enrollment; as a matter of fact, if you did not get to class on time, you might not even get a seat. That was how crowded it was. I was beyond excited and put my whole self into studying and was hoping to be able to finish once and for all. This school was a little different, and classes were tough. Some classes I had to retake because it was a different state and requirements for classes were a little different, but I was determined. That was when another one of my dreams came true. I became pregnant with my second daughter. After she was born, we could no longer afford the tuition for school, so once again, my schooling was put on hold.

Eight-year-old daughters must be the magic ingredient to go to school because when Nadine was eight, my life changed big-time. First, we bought a home, and I was working full-time in a Seasons Resort and country club, Pete had a good job, Claudette had graduated college and was working for American Red Cross and had her own apartment, Marcy had just gotten accepted into the college of her choice, Jackie and Nadine were doing well in school, and best of all, Sammy announced we were going to be grandparents.

Life was good.

Then to my surprise, Seasons got sold and a new crew of people took over, and there was a mass layoff. While collecting unemployment, I was offered an opportunity to go to school to learn a trade. That was when the desire to go back to court reporting school crept back up. After investigating different alternatives, I was able to enroll into court reporting school with the help of unemployment and also a loan to make up the difference I started back at school. I was able to enroll into StenoTech Career Institute my heart and soul into my studies. I practiced night and day on my stenographic machine and also had, by this time, custody of Jackie, as well as Nadine, so my schedule consisted of driving them to afterschool activities and cooking and cleaning, but Pete was a good help when he came home from work.

During the time when I was going to school, my insecurities about my intelligence came back to haunt me. My twin, Bernadette, was also going to school during the same time period. She was attending dental technician school. During one tough week of testing, I rushed to class to see the list of students who passed the test and then would be moved on to the next level. Once again, my name was not listed. I did not pass any of them. I was so depressed and was thinking maybe I should just give up and get a full-time job and forget about being a court reporter. I barely slept, tormented by my inability to pass the test at school regardless of how hard I studied and practiced.

The next day was Bernadette's graduation day from her school. As I sat at the ceremony, I felt like I went back in time to when we were in grade school where she was always excelling and I was always struggling. I put on my best smile, holding back the tears of frustration of my failures of the week when the dean of her school mentioned that there were only two students who made the dean's list, and of course, Bernadette was one of them. As everyone applauded her success, I felt like I was kicked in the stomach. I tried really hard to be happy for her and proud of her, but it was so very hard. I managed to hold back the tears until I was alone in the car. I cried and I prayed.

"Oh God," I prayed, "please give me a sign. Why am I failing while Bernadette is excelling? Should I give up school and get another job? Should I give up on my dream of becoming a court reporter? Please I need a sign. What should I do?"

Monday morning was test day. I reflected back on Bernadette's graduation night and thought, *This is it. I would put a timeline on my progress. If I didn't start passing the test, then I would give up on my dream and get a full-time job doing something else.* There were three tests on that day, one at 180 wpm literary, then 180 wpm Q & A, and the final test, which was always the hardest, 180 medical testimony. After the tests were over, I, along with my fellow classmates, commented on how hard they were, and we laughed, "Better luck next week."

On Tuesday morning, I got to school and cautiously went to the room where the list of students who passed the test was posted. I could not believe my eyes. I truly believe God wanted me to know this was his sign to continue because not only was my name on the list, but my name was the ONLY one on the list. I had passed all three of the tests, allowing me to move to the next level. From that day forward, I progressed along with the other students, moving up the levels, hoping to be able to finish school within a couple of months.

But that was not to happen. On April 14, I had to have an emergency hysterectomy, causing me to miss ten weeks of school. Thankfully, I had a friend, Adeline, who was nice enough to record my academic classes, but I was not able to take the skills test and move on to the faster levels.

After recovering from the hysterectomy, I returned to school, and I was informed by the Director of StenoTech, Mrs. Melone, that I had to start going on job interviews because the unemployment contract was expiring. We both knew I was not ready to get a job in the field, but at least, I was satisfying the contract by going on an interview. There was a request by Bergen County Special Services for a CART provider in a school in Midland Park to work with students with hearing loss. At least, I would get experience going on interviews, so off I went and met with Kathleen Treni, Principal of Hearing Impaired Program for Bergen County Special Services.

"Hi," she said, "I have already interviewed eleven applicants, and I have two more interviews tomorrow. What I am looking for is a person who is trained as a court reporter to be a CART (Communication Access Realtime Translation) Provider, which was to write in real time whatever the teachers would be saying so the students with hearing loss could follow along. This has not been done before in an elementary or high school level in New Jersey, so it was a pilot program and to see how it would work out."

I was so interested in what she was saying and was thinking about when I was ready to graduate. This was the type of job I would look for. I was so calm on the interview because I believed I would not be considered since I was not even close to graduating. I asked tons of questions with the thought that when I was finished with school, this seemed so much more interesting than being a court reporter.

The next morning, I received a call to come back for a second interview. To everyone's surprise, especially mine, I was offered the position.

When I went back to StenoTech and told Mrs. Melone that I was offered the position, I could see the panic in her eyes. After all, I would be representing the school, and we both knew I was nowhere near ready to be out working. She decided to help me by assigning one of the teachers, Marie Kanter, to work one on one with me. At this time, I didn't even know how to put on a laptop. She taught me all about the laptop, as well as taught me how to work the Eclipse Program, and also, I got in touch with a working CART provider, Colleen, who had previously spoken at the school as a guest speaker to assist me in having the Bergen County Special Services purchase the equipment needed to start the job on September 1, 1999. She also advised that I not take the job because it didn't appear I was ready.

Ignoring everyone's opinion, on September 1, 1999, I started my dream job. So much more than a job, I was starting my *career*. No. I was not going to be a court reporter like I always strived for; this was even better. I was going to be a CART provider. Instead of recording rapes, murders, and other court hearings, I would be assisting in students' education. *Wow*, what a great career.

Years after I started my career, I heard Joel Osteen, a TV pastor/ motivational speaker.

He said, "If ever something wonderful happened to you and there was no earthly explanation for how it happened, then that was the hand of God. God not only gives you what you prayed for. He upgrades you."

That is how I look at it. My dream was always to be a court reporter, but being a CART provider was definitely an upgrade.

For the next nineteen years, I worked as a CART provider for Bergen County Special Services first sixteen years in the sixth grade and then three years in the high school. Within one year of my starting as a CART provider; it was decided that the pilot program was going to work, so Kathleen Treni asked if I knew of another CART provider who would be interested in working for Bergen County Special Services. I immediately called Adeline, my friend, who had helped record my classes when I had the hysterectomy. She got the job. When she first told Mrs. Melone, at first, Jean thought it was to replace me, but when Adeline said it was in addition to me, Jean invited me to come back to the school and talk to the students about a career of CART provider. Within the next couple of years, six more of StenoTech's students were employed by Bergen County Special Services.

What a wonderful and amazing honor to have been at the beginning of this program that started as a one-year pilot program and is now, nineteen years later, a successful program that has helped hundreds of students with hearing loss with their education.

In 2002, News 12 New Jersey came to our school to interview me and three students regarding the use of CART and how it helped with their studies; it was quite exciting to watch myself on TV. Also, that same year, I started my own business, See What They're Saying, and registered with the States of New Jersey and New York. As well as working full-time at the school, I worked my business as a CART provider, assisting students in colleges, as well as corporate meetings and religious setting in the evenings and during summers.

Even though we were raised to never be conceited and pat our own back, I can't help but be proud of my accomplishments. I guess all the struggles of the past caused me to persevere.

The Worst Week of Our Life

December 11, 2015, was a day that no parent should ever live through. I stood in the middle of the waiting room at Morristown Memorial Hospital watching our four children being comforted by their spouses and my son-in-law, Bob, holding on to his children for support in their shared grief. My husband and his sister Olga tried unsuccessfully to console each other. The pain was so severe. There I stood all along. After all, I was just the stepmother. Why would anyone think I might need comforting.

Sammy was forty-five years old, Pete's oldest daughter and my stepdaughter for the past thirty-one years. Our relationship was quite rocky, especially in the beginning. When I met Pete, she was fifteen years old and quite a handful. Sammy was born with cerebral palsy; the damage was in her lower extremities, where she had difficulty walking. She had had several surgeries to help her walk with braces. When she was four, her parents divorced while Pete was in the Marines. After having custody of Sammy for two years, Pete's ex-wife, Lucy, decided being a mom of a handicapped child was too hard and asked Pete to agree to have Sammy placed in a state-run facility. He, of course, refused. At this time, Pete was stationed in Japan and immediately got emergency leave. He came back to New Jersey to retain custody of Sammy and asked his sister to care for Sammy until his overseas tour was over. At that time, he retained custody and took her with him to North Carolina while he finished his time in the service.

Being a single dad was pretty rough, especially being in the service and caring for her medical needs. Their relationship was so close, and for the next couple of years, he was at her side with McDonalds in hand as she awoke from one surgery after another. Even after he remarried and had two more children with his second wife, his bond with Sammy was unbreakable.

He was constantly amazed at her desire to do everything her friends did, from riding a bike to playing the softball team with her friend Donna. Of course, not everyone shared in her excitement to join their team. Over and over, Pete had to tell Sammy that because of insurance purposes, she could not play on the team. Sammy was also one of the first handicapped children to be mainstreamed into regular classes.

I never loved him more than I did on the day of her graduation from grammar school. He cried so hard with pride as she walked along with her classmate to get her diploma at St Joseph's Church. He cried so hard that the priest had someone bring him water during the ceremony.

That was not the only time emotions got the best of Pete. On October 8, 1994, Sammy married the man of her dreams, Bob. The wedding was so beautiful, and he held it together pretty well in the church as he walked her down the aisle, but during the father and daughter dance, the DJ stopped the music midway, while Pete composed himself enough to go on. Most fathers and daughters get teary-eyed, as well as the guest during the dance, but Pete was literally sobbing.

During the next couple of years, Sammy and Pete were inseparable. They both had their love of old cars, and during her high school years when other girls were at the mall with their friends, she was in the garage with her dad rebuilding a 1968 Camaro, the same one that her husband and children drove to her funeral in.

On August 5, 2015, while at a BBQ at our home celebrating my brother Raymond's sixtieth birthday, Sammy told us that she was going to have a surgery because she was having difficulty keeping her balance and her doctor said there was a shunt he could insert in her brain to reduce fluid on the brain. Pete was pretty much against the surgery, but she was adamant about having it because she didn't want to always be stuck in a wheelchair all the time. Both Sammy and her husband, Bob, had met with the doctors who assured them this was routine surgery and would improve her mobility.

On October 16, 2015, Sammy had the surgery to insert a shunt to assist in helping control the fluid in her brain, and by all accounts, the doctors were so encouraged about how well the surgery was. Sammy was transferred to Kessler rehab in just one week and was making wonderful progress in healing.

And on November 3, she surprised her daughter Liz at the high school when she was inducted into the National Honor Society.

On November 16, while we were at her son's football game, she started to mention that she had a headache. She described it as "brain freeze," when you eat ice cream too fast. My husband suggested she call the doctor from the field, thinking maybe he would prescribe something to help with the headache. Instead, the doctor told her to go home, and he sent a nurse to her home to take a picture of the incision where they discovered her incision was not healing and he suggest she come back to the hospital to have another staple put in to close the incision.

On Monday after work, I went to visit Sammy at the hospital, expecting her to be in bed since they had taken her into the OR that morning to put in another staple to close the incision. To my surprise, when I got there. She was dressed and waiting to be discharged. There was a decision that she would be fine by giving her antibiotics to take at home to avoid infection.

Within two days, she was back at the hospital with high fever and unable to keep down food. For the next three weeks, she was hospitalized, sometimes in intensive care, then moved into a regular room. We never knew what to expect when visiting her. The night before Thanksgiving, she was sitting up, talking about what kind of pie she wanted us to bring up from home. We were all so thankful she was doing well. However, just as we were sitting down to Thanksgiving dinner the next day, we received a call from the hospital that they were doing emergency surgery to remove the shunt because of widespread infection.

The following two weeks was a nightmare. Some days she would know us, and some days she would just stare into space. The doctors tried convincing us that they were getting the infection under control and she should be home before the holidays. The last time I heard her speak was on my birthday, December 6. I was in the shower when my son-in-law called my phone and put it up to her mouth and left a message.

She breathlessly said, "Happy birthday Bernice," which is a gift to have, and I replay it on my birthday every year since she passed.

What a horrible day December 8 was. Marcy had been eight weeks pregnant when the doctors discovered they could no longer hear a heartbeat and she needed to have a DNC. Because of all that was going on with Sammy, she didn't want to tell us, but her husband felt we should know. We were literally in the car on our way to go see Marcy when we got a call that Sammy had been unresponsive earlier but was now awake.

One of the hardest things in the world is to try to be there for both your children when it is virtually impossible. Thankfully, it was a decision we did not have to make. John called immediately after we received the call from Bob about Sammy and said Marcy's procedure was over, but she was quite tired, so we should not come so she could rest.

We went back to be with Sammy, and she was sleeping peacefully, and the doctors told Bob and us to go home. She would probably sleep the rest of the night.

Suffering from emotional exhaustion, we collapsed without even eating dinner.

At 5:00 a.m. on December 9, a call came from Bob. Sammy had stopped breathing and was on a ventilator.

At 3:00 p.m. that afternoon, we were joined by Bob and a team of doctors who explained that this was so unexpected, but Sammy was showing no signs of brain activity and maybe we should think about taking her off life support. It is a decision no husband or parent should ever have to make. Bob and Pete were at a loss, and I called all the other siblings to the hospital so they could say their goodbyes. Inasmuch as Marcy was having a really hard time herself, we could not keep her from the hospital. Sammy's children, Liz (sixteen) and Eli (fourteen), were bought to the hospital, and suddenly, one of the doctors came in and said he would like to do one more scan to be sure, which would not be until Friday. We were all so hopeful that maybe she would come out of it. We cried and prayed and clung together as a family all the next day, and then again, everyone was there on Friday morning when they took Sammy for the final scan. Pete begged our parish priest to come and pray with us, even though the hospital was an hour away he came. We heard stories from other people in the waiting room how they knew of people who came out of comas and were fine. The extended family was called, and Pete's sister, who cared for Sammy when she was little, booked a flight from Florida and was on her way.

Sammy was bought back to the room, but no doctor came to see us for what seemed like an eternity. All thirteen of us sat holding our breaths when the doctor came in and said, "I'm sorry, there is no brain activity." He said something to the effect if the decision to remove her from life support was too hard to make, she be moved to a nursing home.

Of course, this was Bob's decision as her husband, but out of respect for Pete, he did not want to make it alone. Pete wanted to wait for his sister to arrive before anything was done. For the next couple of hours, we took turns sitting with Sammy saying our private goodbyes. After Olga arrived and the doctors met with Bob and Pete for the final arrangement, it was time.

We stood around the bed not exactly sure what to do. We held hands and said a prayer for Sammy, then the brothers-in-law said their little piece and one by one left the room, then our daughters and son said their goodbyes to her and held each other as they left the room. Olga nearly collapsed as she cried, and I helped her out of the room, leaving Pete, Bob, and the kids with Sammy. A couple of minutes went by when Bob brought Liz and Eli out to the waiting room. He came over to me and asked if I would please get Pete. Bob told me he wanted to be alone with Sammy when she passed, but Pete was showing no signs of leaving her side. I went and guided Pete out of the room, which was no easy feat. He asked to be alone, saying no one knows how he feels, which of course was true, and I hope never to know how he feels.

Not too long later, Bob came out of Sammy's room and said, "She's gone. She took her last breath at 11:11."

I will never forget the image of us leaving the hospital: Liz pushing an empty wheelchair out to the car. Not one person saying anything.

The next day was a whirlwind of people coming over bringing food and offering their condolences and the kids looking at pictures reminiscing, getting ready to put the poster boards together for the funeral home. I, on the other hand, spent the day making phone calls to family and friends repeating over and over the scenario of the last few days, always ending with "She took her last breath at 11:11."

I was on the phone with my brother John, who was not aware that Sammy was even in the hospital. When I told him what happened, he listened silently until I finally I ended the conversation by saying Sammy took her last breathe at 11:11.

He quickly said, "*Oh my god*, you're not going to believe this." He went on to say that he and his wife, Kathy, had been to a flea-market type of thing the day before when a Gypsy lady came to him and asked if 1111 meant anything to him. He said I got married on January 1, 2011, but she said not that. She gave him five pins with number 1111 on them and said something about when a person passes on either 11/11 or at 11:11; the angels came for them. John said he thought she was nuts and tried to get away from her, but she kept following him. At the time, it meant nothing to him, but since Sammy passed at 11:11, it meant she was greeted by angels. Also, five pins were surprising: one for Bob, Liz, Eli, me, and my husband, Pete.

Nothing can take away the pain of losing Sammy, but it was somewhat comforting to my husband when John repeated what happened to him.

Marcy also was looking for anything that would make her feel better; it was quite a tough week for her also, more so than the others. She had lost a baby as well as a sister. At the funeral, she spoke up and said Sammy used to always talk about wanting to be an aunt and that she constantly hinted to her sisters and brother that since Bob was an only child, it was up to them to make her an aunt. After all, she would often joke, "I'm the only one in the family that is not an aunt."

"Well," Marcy said, "now, she is an aunt to my angel baby."

Our week of sorrow was not over yet. We buried Sammy on Wednesday, and then on Friday, we took our cat, Jack, who had been a Father's Day gift from Nadine thirteen years prior, to the vet because he was not able to hold down any food, and the vet recommended we put him down, so in one week, we lost a daughter, a grandbaby, and a pet.

How we made it through that week is still a mystery to me.

Lucky Lady

There was a time in my life where I would have said if it was not for bad luck, I would have no luck at all. Well, times have changed, and yes, I still have some bad luck at times, such as in the case of being a CART provider. The one thing you need for sure is your hands. Well, in nineteen years of being a CART provider, I broke my left arm twice and my right arm once and also had to have six stitches in my index finger. All bad luck, yes, but the first time I got lucky was when I was planting a tree in my backyard in July, I tripped over a shovel, but the cast was removed in time to return to the job in September. The second time was during a school picnic at the end of the school year, so once again, I was without a cast by the time school opened. And the third time was during a school field trip to the bowling alley, so my salary was covered under workmen's compensation. And in the case of the stitches, I was able to purchase a hard plastic covering for the finger, which did not interfere with my job. So I do consider myself a lucky lady even when bad luck is involved.

I definitely do like the casino.

My reasoning for going to the casino, whether right or wrong, was always that I worked so hard, therefore, I should be able to have some fun. So I would take about $100, maybe $150, and try to turn it into something more. I used to call it panic gambling. If I had $75 and it would not be enough to pay a bill, I would think, "Let's see if I can win enough to pay some bills." And as luck would have it, very often I did.

Once on November 1, when I was working, there was a water main break at the school, and we were sent home. I had $55 in cash and $35,00 free play, so I decided to go to the casino. I won $1,288 on a penny machine and quickly left. I went straight home and called the oil company, ordered a full tank of oil, then went to the super-market and bought a bunch of groceries.

On another occasion, in 2012, my daughter Nadine was getting married, I was working so many side jobs and a full-time job to help pay for the wedding. I was making payments along with Nadine and her future in-laws for the Tides, and I also was single-handedly pay-ing off her $1,300 dress and veil. The weekend before Nadine was coming home from college for her final dress fitting, I was panicking because I still owed $242 on the dress and knew I could not squeeze it out of the bill money. I took $60 from the account and headed for the casino, where I also had $30 free play. I went to my favorite one-penny machine and played for about half hour. After a couple of hits, I realized I had $250 in the machine. I cashed out and headed home, so excited that I had enough for the final payment on the dress.

Also on the day my daughter moved with her new husband to North Carolina, I was quite upset and was sitting feeling down when my girlfriend called and said she was taking a ride to the Sands and was wondering whether I wanted to come. Of course, it did not take much convincing on her part. I took $100 and had $60 in free play, and an hour before we were had agreed on leaving, I won $1,900 playing only a penny machine.

Then on December 17, 2014, I was on my way to my college job when I got a call from my student informing me class was can-celled so I decided that I would go to the casino for a little downtime. I had been working fulltime job, two nights a week and every other Saturday, so I just wanted to relax and enjoy. When I got there, I noticed someone was on my favorite machine, and being a creature of habit, I decided to get a bite to eat rather than go on another machine. When I finished eating, my machine was free. I put in a $20 and started to play the maximum bet, which was $3, which I usually never did, but I had just gotten paid from my job. I was feeling pretty lucky, and it had been a while since I had been there. I immediately won $375, and after a couple more spins, I won $375 again, and before I knew it, I was over $1,100. I did not want to put the money back and started to think of all the bills I could pay and Christmas gifts I could buy, so I made up my mind. I would play it down to $1,000, and then I would stop and cash out. I reasoned that thirty-three times at $3 is $99, so I started to count, and at thirty-one, the machine lit up, and I won $8,762.37 jackpot. Wow, this was crazy.

In June, our granddaughter was being christened, and Pete's brother and sister-in-law from North Carolina came to stay with us for a week. My sister-in-law Judy also enjoyed the casino, so to entertain her while she was visiting, we went up to the casino. Our plan was to leave at six o'clock and go home in time for a nice dinner with the guys. While I was waiting at the exit, I put a $20 in a machine I never tried before, playing $1.50. After a couple of hits, a man sitting next to me informed me that I hit a feature. Not sure what I was looking for, I turned to ask what was the feature, and the man suddenly yelled, "Hey, look, you hit the jackpot." I won $13,878.34.

The casino is not the only place where I consider myself a lucky lady On October 26, both Bernadette's and my children were throwing me and Bernadette a surprise birthday party at the firehouse. It turned out Nadine made up an excuse that her mother-in-law, Caryn, was inviting me and Bernadette to a psychic at her house and we had to be there by three thirty, which was cutting it close since I got out of the job I was working at one and it took two hours to get home from all the way down in Mercer County.

I drove like a crazy person to get there in time, and when I was just about five minutes away, Caryn called to say her husband did not feel well so instead come to the firehouse where she was holding the physic reading because she did not want me and Bernadette getting sick. Well, I picked Bernadette up and got to the firehouse just in time for 107 people to scream, "HAPPY BIRTHDAY!"

It was about six weeks too early, but it was the BEST DAY OF MY LIFE, other than the birth of both my daughters.

At the end of the party, Pete and I was asked to come to the back of the room for a little surprise. It turned out that our children did not acknowledge our anniversary, which was in August. It kind of hurt our feelings, but we soon learned why. All of our five children and their spouses chipped in to send us on a cruise.

I am not only a lucky lady, but I am truly blessed.

Madison's Christening

June 16, 2018, what a beautiful day for a christening. Madison, our precious granddaughter, born to Marcy and her husband, John, was being christened, and at the ceremony and party to follow were all the usual suspects, like my husband and me and our children and their spouses, along with our other granddaughter Liz, who was the godmother, and grandson Eli, and of course, the grandparents on the other side, as well as friends and extended family.

What made this celebration unusual was some of the guests, which included Pete's ex-wife, Brooke, and her present husband, Dennis, as well as her second ex-husband, Billy, as well as her brother Artie, whom Pete had not seen since his nasty divorce from Brook.

As anyone knows, during divorces, most people are at their worse, exaggerating things to make their story seem worse in the eyes of the court, and Pete's divorce was no different than most.

There were accusations of cheating and also gambling and also constant fights over everything, including who should have custody of the children.

Anyone with any brains would have seen this as a crazy situation and not have walked away from this situation, she would have RUN, but I guess that's why they say LOVE IS BLIND.

Shortly after we started dating, Brook met and married Billy. Husband number two was a little older and appeared to be stable, and Brook pleaded with Pete to allow her to have the children back. Feeling it would be best for the children, since his older daughter Sammy grew up without her mom, he did not want the same thing to happen for his younger children; he reluctantly agreed. At first, things were fine. We visited with the children one night a week, as well as every other weekend. Pete had his own home with Sammy, and I had my own apartment with my daughter Claudette.

Gradually, Brook started to change the schedule of our visits, and then when Pete sold his house, he and I moved together with both daughters into an apartment. Then she started causing problems.

Brooke started to alter our visitation schedule with almost no notice causing many arguments between Pete and myself.

On one occasion, we were celebrating my daughter Claudette's eighth-grade graduation with a party. The children were due to be returned to their mom by 9:00 p.m. Pete called and said we would be dropping them off a little late because we were waiting for our guest to leave the party.

When we arrived, we were greeted at the door by her husband, Billy, shouting at us that they were so upset. Apparently, Brooke did not tell him about Pete's phone call explaining our reason for bringing the kids home late. Pete and Billy got into an argument, and Billy shoved him, causing Pete to fall backward down the stairs. Needless to say, the fight got worse, and the cops were called. Brook denied she received Pete's call, explaining our bringing the kids home late and tried to get his visitation stopped. We needed to get a lawyer, and things only got worse.

For the next couple of years, we were in and out of court numerous times with false accusations.

The judge sided with us and told him that he was not to interfere with Pete's rights as the children's father.

After that court appearance, we all had to be civilized with one another. Over the next few years, we attended events relating to the children, such as communion, confirmation, and graduations. All strained and a little uncomfortable but civilized all for the benefit of the children.

Now here we are, thirty-two years after starting this blended family, attending this beautiful baby's christening. Who would have guessed this little girl could bring so many people together and all get along?

Billy also attended the christening because he maintained a relationship with Marcy and Jackie after his divorce from their mom.

As we all posed for a group picture, I wondered how the judge and lawyers would react to see this picture.

We are living proof that blended families can work with a lot of hard work and keeping in mind always the children's best interest.

Random Acts of Kindness

As the time for retiring is approaching, I can't help but stop and look back on the random acts of kindness given to me by so many people. I often wonder if someone's good deeds are realized as being as important from the person doing it as to the person receiving it. My intention is to somehow thank the people who have helped me along the way because, as I look back over my years of work, I have to say I definitely would not have succeeded without the random acts of kindness.

In 1981, I was so excited at the prospect of going to court reporting school, which would never have happened had it not been for the generosity of my brother, John, who paid my first tuition payment.

Also, being a single mother and being financially responsible for all the bills—which included rent, food, and electricity and catholic school expenses for myself and my daughter—there was little money left from my job to spend on extras. Although my tuition was paid for court reporting school, the other expenses—such as textbooks, stenographic machine and paper, bus fare to and from school, as well as an evening babysitter—was present. How was I ever going to be able to do all this was a constant worry, but with the kindness of so many, my dream became a reality.

I would like to acknowledge with the hopes that the persons who have helped will recognize their act of kindness and realize they made a substantial difference in my life.

On the first day of school, I was given a list of all the items I would need to be able to proceed in my studies. First, being a steno-graphic machine, with tripod, then several textbooks and paper. Due to the fact the course was so hard and it definitely was not for everyone, the school had a program where you could rent the machine for the first three months, which was good because there was no way I could afford to purchase one outright, but the textbooks was another story. You had to purchase them; it just so happened the payment for my textbooks was due exactly the same time my daughter's book bill was due. So of course, as any good parent does, I paid her bill, that meant that I could look on with another student during class but did not have access to do the homework assignments. One of my class-mates, Christine Vergona, realized I hadn't purchased my own book, so without asking, she was nice enough to photocopy the pages at her dad's shop that I needed to do the homework assignments until I had saved enough to get my own book. That little gesture made it possible for me to keep up with my studies.

Shortly thereafter, I had mentioned, when class was running over, that I had to leave because I was going to miss my bus back to Jersey City. The following week at school, one of my classmates asked if I had a car, and I said no. She then said that the bus stop was not exactly a safe area of town, so she would drive me to the bus stop and wait with me in the car until my bus came. A few days later, I was introduced to two students from Jersey City, Connie and Lisa, who offered to drive me so I didn't need to take the bus. When I tried to pay, both girls refused, saying they had to go anyway. Of course I did pay for gas, occasionally.

When the three-month rental of the machine expired, I was in a jam because I had not saved enough for the new machine. That's when my sister-in-law, Barbara, talked to her aunt—who was a retired court reporter—and she was nice enough to give me her machine. It was not as modern as the ones at school, but it certainly did the trick, and also threw in a box of paper, saving me even more money, and would not take any money. She just made me promise I would study like crazy because, as she said, it's a hard course and not for everybody.

True to her word, the course to become a court reporter was quite difficult, and little by little, the classes got smaller and smaller—with many students dropping out—that eventually the school had no choice but to end their evening classes, leaving me brokenhearted because there was no way for me to transfer to the day classes.

About two years later, I once again was able to go back to court reporting school. No, my finances were not much better, but my desire to go back to school was there, so I was determined to make it work. By this time, my daughter was ten, still not old enough to be home in the evenings alone, but I was lucky enough to have a friend who would babysit for Claudette on my school nights, and I would babysit for her kids when she and her husband wanted to go out, with no money changing hands.

Everything seemed to fall into place. I got out of work from my day job in Jersey City at 4:00 p.m., and the school started at six thirty in Hackensack, and lucky for me, the bus stop was right up the corner from my job, and also, there was a little donut shop called King Donut right at the bus stop, so it became my habit to have a little something to eat there on Mondays and Thursdays—often studying while there. On one occasion, a week when Claudette had been invited to a birthday party, I had spent what little money I had on a gift for her friend, so instead of ordering food, I just ordered coffee. When the owner of the shop came over and asked why I wasn't eating, I just said, "Oh, I'm not hungry," and he said, "What time do you get out of class?"

I replied, "Nine thirty."

He said, "Okay," and came back with a cheesesteak, which was one of my favorites, and said, "you won't do well in class if you don't have a full stomach. Let's make a deal. You eat on Monday and Thursday and pay when you get paid. No sense paying to go to school and fail 'cause you can't concentrate."

So for the next couple of months, it would go on like this; then one day, I stopped in to pay my bill and was told it was paid. Apparently, an older gentleman, who was a steady customer, asked about me and said he thought it was great to want to better myself and wanted to continue paying for my meals but did not want to be identified.

As my daughter got older, so did the expenses—such as braces— and at one point, she needed eye surgery, which was not completely covered under my insurance. So as much as I didn't want to, I had made the decision to drop out of school because I could not make the tuition payments any longer. I owed $300, and then the next payment was almost due to take me till the end of the last semester. During a break at school, I had mentioned to my fellow classmates that I would be dropping out the following week. Two of my classmates were two religious nuns from St. Al's High School, who were taking the course because they wanted to introduce it as an option for their seniors at the high school.

A few days later, I received a notice from the court reporting school, stating my tuition was paid for the rest of the semester by an anonymous donor, and till this day, I still do not know who paid it, but the more help I received, the harder I studied—grateful beyond belief.

Even later on in life as I worked as a CART provider the kindness of others was apparent and so appreciated. I worked many nights providing CART Services at colleges that were located at least one hour away from my home and I had two wonderful coworkers, Lynn and Barbara from Midland Park who would offer me to spend the night at their homes during inclement weather or even just if my classes got out late. The support and inspiration I received from both people I knew and complete strangers, people whom I will never know, is what has kept me going when the going got rough. It took me a total of eighteen years to realize my dream, but I know that I would not have made it without others cheering me along the way. Whenever I would not do well on a test or even failed the certification test more times than I care to say, I had family and friends—especially a few cousins—who would lift my spirits and keep reminding me how I could do it. And to each and every one of these people, I want to say, "I owe my success to you."

For with every act of kindness, there is a recipient whose life can be forever changed.

My Time to Retire

Looking back over my life, I realized my life was really not the normal run-of-the-mill, predictable life.

Let's see, I was a twin, one of ten children, a teenage mom, battered wife, single mom, a second wife, a stepmom, and a new mom at the age of thirty-five, then a grandmother at the age of forty-five. I was published eight times and on TV twice. I realized my dream and started a career as a CART provider after struggling in court reporting school on and off for eighteen years, becoming the first CART provider to work in middle school and high school in all of New Jersey, then started my own business, SEE WHAT THEY'RE SAYING, and had the extreme privilege of providing CART services in colleges, law schools, many corporate functions, synagogues, churches, for funerals and weddings, also at Madison Square Garden, United Nations, and Carney Hall.

I started to think seriously about retiring. Not that I didn't like my job, I certainly did, but I was getting tired of working so much, and I also was thinking about my three brothers who had passed away. Each one was in their early seventies, and also two of my sisters had been diagnosed with cancer, one with pancreatic and one with liver, and it made me think about myself and how I had worked hard all my life, and I wanted to have some downtime before I was either too sick to enjoy life or even worse. I know that with my pension and Pete's pension plus our both social security checks, we would be able to make ends meet, and with my business, I would still be able to make extra money when needed, but it would be at my discretion.

So my plans began, and retirement was on my mind, and I started to count down the days, even keeping a list with my days numbered. I saved money and planned my own retirement party and planned the menu and hired a DJ so everyone that came could have a good time. I asked that there be no speeches like was usual in retirement parties that I have been to, even though I myself gave speeches at three retirement parties of my coworkers. I felt I would not be comfortable with anyone speaking on my behalf, and I didn't want any of my friends to feel they were expected to say anything. I was so excited about my party I even made my own invitation.

JANUARY 1ST IS THE OFFICIAL DATE
BUT
NOVEMBER 24TH AT 3PM IS WHEN
WE WILL CELEBRATE
AT
HIGHLAND LAKES FIREHOUSE
813 Canistear Rd
Highland Lakes, NJ 07422

PLEASE RSVP BY 11/1/18
FIRSTCART1999@JUNO.COM

On November 24, 2018, I realized a dream that I held for so many years. I celebrated with 101 friends and family the end of my working career and the beginning of my freedom, and it also occurred to me, looking back on my unusual life, one that was like no other, it was evident at this time, not only was I ready to retire, but I DAMN WELL EARNED IT. And I look forward to enjoying it.

About the Author

Bernice Bonilla is one of ten children born and raised in Jersey City, New Jersey. She has two daughters, two stepdaughters, one stepson, and three grandchildren. She lives in Highland Lakes with her husband, Pete. She is a retired CART provider and is the sole proprietor of See What They're Saying.

CPSIA information can be obtained
at www.ICGtesting.com
Printed in the USA
LVHW031207100221
678885LV00004BA/692